BEGINNER
coursebook

Kate Pickering & Jackie McAvoy

series author Lindsay Clandfield

MACMILLAN

About Global

Kate Pickering is the director of the Adults' Department at International House, Madrid. There she combines running a large department with her work as a teacher trainer and assessor on Cambridge CELTA and DELTA as well as IH's in-service training programmes. She continues to teach regularly and particularly enjoys working with low level students such as the senior learners she taught while writing Global Beginner and Elementary.

Jackie McAvoy is a teacher, teacher-trainer and educational materials writer. She also produces podcasting material for learners and teachers of English. Jackie has worked in many different countries including Spain, Vietnam and Jordan. Her first published book was *Essential Reading* for Macmillan Education.

Six things we wanted for global

real lives

international voices

intellectual curiosity

cultural knowledge

a global outlook

a different book

Global Beginner by numbers:

15 units 128 pages 37 texts about people and places from around the world 32 vocabulary sections 27 explanations of English grammar 11 functional language lessons 21 accents from around the world in Global Voices 229 audio clips 30 video clips 150 interactive activities 100s of curious and interesting facts

Content highlights

1 **Name** & **Address**
Introducing yourself
Postcode
Common English words

2 **Me** & **You**
Countries and nationalities Four women from around the world Interview with Luis Ruiz

3 **Them** & **Us**
1000 families
Family numbers
A family photograph

4 **Big** & **Small**
Shopping in numbers
A small shop near my house

5 **Work** & **Play**
VSO Describing jobs
Sports The Human Race

6 **Day** & **Night**
A day in my life
24/7 services

7 **Places** & **People**
UNESCO World Heritage sites
Great Smoky Mountains National Park On safari

8 **In** & **Out**
Eating in, Cuban style
Going out in London

9 **Here** & **There**
Living underground
48 hours in Vancouver

10 **Ancient** & **Modern**
Ancient civilizations ... the Khmer & the Maya
Cairo

11 **Life** & **Times**
DNA man ... the biography of Francis Crick Around the world in 2004

12 **Question** & **Answer**
The Southern Day frog Tribes
The TV series: Tribes

13 **Business** & **Pleasure**
EuroStar in numbers A business trip
Moscow A bus tour of Moscow

14 **Arts** & **Technology**
Wall paintings Two paintings One laptop per child

15 **Language** & **Learning**
Jersey A Papua New Guinea language

Contents

		Grammar	Reading and Listening texts	Vocabulary	Speaking, Pronunciation and Functional language
UNIT 1	**Name** page 6	Regular plural nouns (p7)	Introducing yourself (p6) The alphabet (p6) Common English words (p7)	Common English words (p7)	The alphabet (p6) Spelling words (p6) (P) Word stress (p7) (FL) Meeting people (p7)
	Address page 8	*What's* (p9)	Numbers 1–10 (p8) Postcodes (p9)	Numbers 1–10 (p8)	(FL) *How are you?* (p8) Filling in a form (p9) (W) Filling in a form (p9)
		Global game (p10)		**Global review** (p11)	
UNIT 2	**Me** page 12	Subject pronouns (p12) *be* (p13) *Yes / no* questions (p13)	Countries and nationalities (p12) Four women from around the world (p13)	Countries and nationalities (p12)	(P) Intonation of *yes/no* questions (p13) (FL) Introducing yourself (p13)
	You page 14	Possessive adjectives (1) (p15)	Interview with Luis Ruiz (p14) Asking questions (p14)	Numbers 11–20 (p15)	Personal details (p15) (W) Personal details (p15)
		Global voices (p16)		**Global review** (p17)	
UNIT 3	**Them** page 18	Possessive adjectives (2) (p19) (W) Describing a family (p19)	Families (p18)	Families (p18)	(P) Linking words (p18) Describing a family (p18)
	Us page 20	Possession (p20) Questions with *be* (p21)	Family numbers (p20) A family photograph (p21)	Family (p20)	Family numbers (p20) Your family (p20) (FL) Introducing people (p21)
		Global reading (p22)		**Global review** (p23)	
UNIT 4	**Big** Page 24	*There is / there are* (p25)	Shopping in numbers (p24) (W) Describing a hotel (p25)	Numbers 20–100 (p24) Shopping in numbers (p24)	(P) Schwa /ə/ (p25)
	Small page 26		A small shop near my house; adjectives (p27)	Prices (p26) A small shop near my house; adjectives (p27)	Prices (p26) (FL) In a shop (p26) A shop near your house (p27) (W) A shop near your house (p27)
		Global game (p28)		**Global review** (p29)	
UNIT 5	**Work** page 30	*There isn't / there aren't* (p30)	VSO (p30) Describing jobs (p30)	Jobs (p31)	Jobs (p31)
	Play page 32	*like* (p33)	Talking about sports (p32) The Human Race (p33)	Sports (p32) Talking about sports (p 32)	Sports (p32) (P) *like* (p33) The Human Race (p33)
		Global voices (p34)		**Global review** (p35)	
UNIT 6	**Day** page 36	Present simple (p37)	Daily routine – *have* and *go* (p36) A day in my life (p37) (W) A day in the life of … (p37)	Daily routine / *have* and *go* (p36)	(FL) Telling the time (p36)
	Night page 38	Present simple negative (p39)	Service 24/7 (p39)	The time (p38) Your favourite time of day (p38) (EV) *good* + time of day (p38)	(P) The time, word stress (p38) Your favourite time of day (p38) (FL) Giving an opinion (p39)
		Global reading (p40)		**Global review** (p41)	
UNIT 7	**Places** page 42	Question words (p43) (W) A place you know (p43)	UNESCO World Heritage sites (p42) Great Smoky Mountains National Park (p43)	Places in nature (p42)	Question words (p43)
	People page 44	Present simple questions (p45)	On safari (p44)	People you know (p44)	A person you know well (p45)
		Global game (p46)		**Global review** (p47)	
UNIT 8	**In** Page 48		Eating in, Cuban style (p49)	Food (p48)	Food (p48) (P) Consonant clusters (p 48) Eating in, Cuban style (p49) (FL) Offering (p49)
	Out page 50	Adverbs of frequency (p51) (W) Eating out (p51)	Time Out (p50)	Days of the week (p50) (EV) *classes* (p50)	(P) Days of the week (p50)
		Global voices (p52)		**Global review** (p53)	

EV – Extend your vocabulary   (P) – Pronunciation   (W) – writing   (FL) – functional language

		Grammar	Reading and Listening texts	Vocabulary	Speaking, Pronunciation and Functional language
UNIT 9	**Here** page 54	Prepositions of place (p55)	Living underground (p55)	Rooms and furniture (p54)	Giving opinions (p55)
	There page 56	Imperatives (p57)	48 hours in Vancouver (p56) Ⓦ 48 hours in Vancouver (p57)	Types of transport (p56) 48 hours in Vancouver (p56)	Types of transport (p56) Ⓟ Sentence stress (p57) ⒻⓁ Making recommendations (p57)
		Global reading (p58)		Global review (p59)	
UNIT 10	**Ancient** page 60	Was / were (p61)	Ancient civilisations (p60) Life in the past (p61) Ⓦ Life in the past (p61)		Ancient civilisations (p60)
	Modern page 62	Was / were negative and questions (p63)	Adjectives (p62) Cairo (p63)	Adjectives (p62)	Ⓟ Stress and intonation (p63) Asking about a trip (1) (p63)
		Global game (p64)		Global review (p65)	
UNIT 11	**Life** page 66	Past simple (p66)	DNA: fact or fiction? (p66) Biography of Francis Crick (p66) Ⓦ A biography / autobiography (p67)	Years and life events (p66)	Ⓟ Regular past simple (p67)
	Times page 68	Past simple negative (p69)	2004 (p68)	Dates (p68)	Talking about last year (p69)
		Global voices (p70)		Global review (p71)	
UNIT 12	**Question** page 72	Past simple questions (p73) Ⓦ The Bali Tiger (p73)	The Southern Day Frog (p72)	Animals (p72)	Animals that disappeared (p73)
	Answer Page 74		Tribes (p74) The TV series Tribe (p75)	Ⓔⓥ time (p75)	Visiting another country (p74) Ⓟ Stress and rhythm (p75) Asking about a trip (2) (p75)
		Global reading (p76)		Global review (p77)	
UNIT 13	**Business** page 78	Present continuous (p79)	Eurostar in numbers (p78) A business trip (p78)	Travelling for business (p78) Eurostar in numbers (p78)	Travelling for business (p78) ⒻⓁ Buying a ticket (p79)
	Pleasure page 80	Present continuous negative and questions (p81) Ⓦ An email to a friend (p81)	Moscow (p80) A bus tour of Moscow (p81)	Tourism (p80)	Moscow (p80) Ⓟ Intonation in questions (p81)
		Global game (p82)		Global review (p83)	
UNIT 14	**Arts** page 84	Describing nouns (p85)	Wall paintings (p84) Two paintings (p85)	Colours (p84)	Two paintings (p85) ⒻⓁ Agreeing and disagreeing (p85)
	Technology Page 86	Can / can't (p87) Ⓦ Linking words (p87)	One laptop per child (p86)	Technology (p86)	What we have (p86) Ⓟ can / can't (p87)
		Global voices (p88)		Global review (p89)	
UNIT 15	**Language** Page 90	Be going to (future) (p91)	Jersey (p90)	Ways of saying numbers (p90) Ⓔⓥ local (p90)	Disappearing languages (p91) Ⓦ A Papua New Guinea language (p91)
	Learning page 92	Language review (p92)	Language learning around the world (p92) The United Kingdom of language learners (p93)		Language learning around the world (p92) Giving a presentation (p93)
		Global reading (p94)		Global review (p95)	

Communication Activities: **Additional Material: (p104)**   **Grammar focus: (p106)**   **Audioscript: (p120)**   **Irregular verbs: (p126)**

Student A: (p96)   **Student B: (p100)**   **Phonetic symbols and alphabet: (p105)**

Name & Address

Part 1

Listening & Speaking
Introducing yourself

Listening & Speaking
The alphabet

Vocabulary & Listening
Common English words

Pronunciation
Word stress

Grammar
Regular plural nouns

Functional language
Meeting people

Listening and Speaking

1 🔊 **1.01** Look at the pictures. Listen and underline *Hi* or *Hello*.

2 🔊 **1.02** Listen and complete the sentences with cities from the box.

Cape Town	London	Mumbai
New York	Sydney	Toronto

3 Complete the sentences about you.
Hi. I'm _____.
I'm from _____.

4 Work in pairs. Read the sentences to your partner.

Listening and Speaking

1 🔊 **1.03** Listen and repeat the letters.

a b c d e f g
h i j k l m n
o p q r s t u
v w x y z

2 🔊 **1.04** Listen and underline the correct words.

Hi, I'm *Leslie / Lesley* …
I'm from *Torquay / Tokyo*.

3 Talk to four students. Write the names and cities of the students.

A: *Hi, I'm Jan.*
B: *Can you spell that?*
A: *J-A-N.*
A: *I'm from Krakow.*
B: *Can you spell that?*
A: *K-R-A-K-O-W.*

1 *Hi / Hello.* I'm Tom. I'm from _____.   2 *Hi / Hello.* I'm Liz. I'm from _____.

4 *Hi / Hello.* I'm Steve. I'm from _____.   5 *Hi / Hello.* I'm Sasha. I'm from _____.   6 *Hi / Hello.* I'm Pam. I'm from _____.

3 *Hi / Hello.* I'm Atul. I'm from _____.

camera

coffee

taxi

bank

bus

passport

book

phone

café

hotel

Vocabulary and Listening

1 1.05 Look at the pictures. Listen and repeat the words.

2 1.06 Read and listen.

A: camera
B: Can you spell that?
A: C-A-M-E-R-A

3 Work in pairs. Spell three words to your partner.

4 Work in pairs. A: turn to page 96. B: turn to page 100. Practise spelling words.

5 1.07 Listen to the names. <u>Underline</u> the incorrect letters.

1 Br<u>a</u>wn
2 Bull
3 Clerk
4 Parker
5 James

Pronunciation

1 1.08 Listen and tick (✔) the correct column.

	●	•●	●•
hi	✔		
hello			
coffee			
phone			
camera			
café			
hotel			
bus			
passport			

2 Listen again and repeat the words.

Grammar

> a book   10 book**s**
> a bus   2 bus**es**
> a city   5 cit**ies**

- to form a regular plural noun add *-s*, *-es* or *-ies*.

Write the plural forms.

a passport   *2 passports*
1 a coffee   2 _____
2 a phone   2 _____
3 a taxi   2 _____
4 a camera   2 _____

Ⓖ **Grammar focus** – explanation & more practice of nouns on page 106

Functional language

1 1.09 Listen and put the sentences in the correct order.

1 Hello Tom. I'm Liz. ___
Nice to meet you, Liz. ___
Hi. I'm Tom. _1_

2 Nice to meet you, Atul. ___
Hello. I'm Sasha. ___
Hi Sasha. I'm Atul. ___

2 Say *hello* to other students in the class.

Useful phrases

- Hello/Hi.
- I'm …
- Nice to meet you.

Name & Address

Part 2

Functional Language
How are you?

Vocabulary & Listening
Numbers 1–10

Reading & Listening
Postcodes

Grammar
What's

Writing & Speaking
Filling in a form

Functional language

1 🔊 1.10 Listen and match the conversations to the pictures.

1 A: How are you?
   B: Fine, thanks. And you?
   A: Great!

2 A: How are you?
   B: OK. And you?
   A: Not bad.

2 Listen again and repeat.

3 Ask other students in the class *How are you?*

Useful phrases

- How are you?
- Fine / Great / OK / Not bad.
- And you?

Vocabulary and Listening

1 🔊 1.11 Listen and repeat the numbers.

2 Match the numbers with the words.

a 1   two
b 2   four
c 3   one
d 4   five
e 5   three
f 6   eight
g 7   six
h 8   ten
i 9   seven
j 10   nine

3 🔊 1.12 Listen and write the numbers. What's the missing number? Write the word.

a _1_ _2_ _3_ _5_   _four_
b __ __ __ __   ____
c __ __ __ __   ____
d __ __ __ __   ____
e __ __ __ __   ____
f __ __ __ __   ____

4 Work in pairs. Say five numbers. Your partner writes the numbers.

5 🔊 1.13 Listen and match 1–5 to the pictures.

6 Listen again and write the numbers.

a Room _ _ _
b Manchester United _
   Liverpool _
c _ _ _ _
d _!_,_–,_–,_–,_–,_!
e _ _ _ _ _ _

Reading and Listening

1 Look at the addresses. Circle the postcodes.

2 🔊 **1.14** Listen and correct the postcodes.

3 Read the text about postcodes. Are the sentences true (T) or false (F)?

1 In Britain the word is *zip code*. ___
2 In Russia the postcode is a number. ___
3 S2 67X is an Australian postcode. ___
4 B6 7TT is a Manchester postcode. ___

> **Language note:**
> use *an* before a vowel sound: *an address*;
> *an Australian postcode*

4 Work in pairs. What's your postcode? Tell your partner.

5 Work in pairs. A: turn to page 96. B: turn to page 100. Practise saying postcodes.

Grammar

> *What's the postcode?*
> *What's your name?*
>
> • use *What's* (what is) to ask about things

1 Complete the questions with the words in the box.

> address   name   phone number
> postcode

1 A: What's your _____?
   B: Paul Jackson.
2 A: What's your _____?
   B: 01202 671150
3 A: What's your _____?
   B: 2 London Street, Manchester.
4 A: What's your _____?
   B: M3 6ST

2 🔊 **1.15** Listen and check.

ⓖ **Grammar focus** – explanation & more practice of *What's* on page 106

• The postcode is part of your address.

• In the US, the word is zip code.

• In Australia, China and Russia the postcode is a number.

• In Britain the postcode is numbers and letters. The first letter is the city: L4 0TH is a Liverpool postcode (Liverpool is L). G53 6XW is a Glasgow postcode (Glasgow is G).

Writing and Speaking

Work in pairs. Ask your partner questions to complete the form. Choose A or B.

A talk about yourself, or

B A: turn to page 96.
    B: turn to page 100.

Name	
Address	
Postcode	
Phone number	

Useful phrases

• What's your name / address / postcode / phone number?
• Can you spell that?
• Can you repeat that?

1
Zhu Chen
74 TianHe North Road
Guangzhou
520651
CHINA

2
Robert Jones
36 St. Pauls Street
Birmingham
B3 1XQ
ENGLAND

3
P. Howe
32 Elginton Avenue
Ontario
L5R 3F8
CANADA   AIR MAIL

4
Chad Baker
262 Peachtree Avenue
Atlanta
GA 30302
POSTAGE PAID AUSTRALIA   USA

5
Oleg Bratersky
71 Smolenskaya Ulitsa
Moscow
119123
RUSSIA

Global game

Start You start!

1 Say a word beginning with *p*
passport

2 Say a drink

3 Say a place

4 Say a country
France

5 Say a city in Britain
London

16 Say a name in English
John, Anna

17 Say a place

18 Say a name in English
Lisa, Peter

19 Say a word beginning with *p*

6 Say a job

15 Say a word beginning with *t*

24 Say a plural noun
cities

25 Say a city in Britain
London

20 Say a place

7 Say a city in the US
Chicago

14 Say a country
Australia

23 Say 3 numbers
three, …

22 Say a name in English
John, Anna

21 Say a word beginning with *b*

8 Say a name in English
John, Anna

13 Say a city in the US
Chicago

12 Say a word beginning with *c*

11 Say 3 numbers
five, …

10 Say a plural noun
cities

9 Say a name in English
Lisa, Peter

It's my / your turn

Global review

Vocabulary

1 Write the numbers as words in the crossword puzzle.

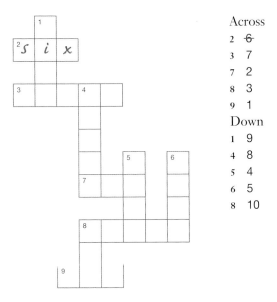

Across
2 6
3 7
7 2
8 3
9 1

Down
1 9
4 8
5 4
6 5
8 10

2 Find nine words. Use the pictures to help you.

c	a	m	e	r	a	w	l
o	h	o	t	e	l	p	b
f	g	u	t	a	x	i	o
f	o	u	r	c	y	f	o
e	p	h	o	n	e	v	k
e	k	c	a	f	e	a	s
p	a	s	s	p	o	r	t

Pronunciation

Tick (✔) the correct column.

	●	●·
taxi		
phone		
café		
bank		
camera		

Grammar

1 Match the questions with the answers.

1 What's your name?
2 Can you spell that?
3 What's your postcode?
4 What's your address?
5 What's your telephone number?

a Yes, M-A-Y-A C-O-X
b 0151 7613 4069
c Maya Cox
d L6 4BY
e 5 Hill Road, Liverpool

2 Write your answers to the questions.

What's your name? _____.
What's your address? _____.
What's your postcode? _____.
What's your telephone number? _____.

Listen again

1 Put the words in the correct order.

Tokyo. from I'm   *I'm from Tokyo.*

1 Tom. I'm Hi,   _____
2 Liz. Tom, I'm Hello   _____
3 you, to Liz. meet Nice _____

2 💿 1.16 Listen and check your answers.

3 💿 1.17 Listen and write the numbers.

a _____
b _____
c _____
d _____
e _____
f _____

Me & You

Part 1

Vocabulary & Listening

Countries and nationalities

Grammar

Subject pronouns; be

Reading & Listening

Four students at the International School of English, London

Grammar

Yes/No questions

Pronunciation & Speaking

Intonation of Yes/No questions

Functional language

Introductions

Vocabulary and Listening

1 Complete the key on the map with the words in the box.

| Spanish | Russian | Chinese | English |

2 🔊 1.18 Listen, check and repeat.

3 Complete the table with the nationalities.

Country	Nationality
Italy	Italian
Russia	_____
Germany	German
Brazil	Brazilian
Egypt	Egyptian

— **-ian / -an**

China	_____
Japan	Japanese
Portugal	Portuguese

— **-ese**

Britain	British
Spain	_____
Poland	Polish

— **-ish**

| France | French |

— **(others)**

4 🔊 1.19 Listen and repeat.

5 🔊 1.20 Listen to the conversations and underline the words you hear.

| Spanish | German | English | French |
| Italian | Polish | Russian | Japanese |

MAJOR LANGUAGES

	1 _____
	2 _____
	3 _____
	ARABIC
	HINDI
	4 _____
	PORTUGUESE
	FRENCH

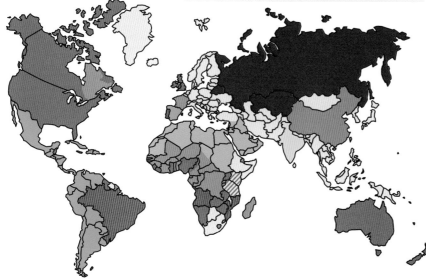

6 Complete the sentences.

Hiroko's from Japan.   *She's Japanese.*
1 Lucian is from England.   He's _____.
2 Maria's from Spain.   She's _____.
3 Olga and Tatiana are   They're _____.
   from Russia.

7 Complete the sentences about you.

I'm from _____. I'm _____.

Grammar

I am / I'm Polish.
You are / You're German.
She, He, It is / She's Spanish.
We are / We're Japanese.
They are / They're Russian.

I am not / I'm not Russian.
She, He, It is not / She isn't Polish.
They are not / They aren't Spanish.

- *am / are / is* etc is the verb *be*
- *I / you / he* etc are subject pronouns
- use subject pronouns before the verb (*am, are, is* etc)
- use *not / n't* for the negative
- use contractions (*I'm, you're, he's* etc) in conversation

1 Complete with subject pronouns.

Tomasz is from Poland. __He__ *is Polish.*
1 Fatima is Egyptian. _____ is from Cairo.
2 I'm Andrei and this is Mikita. _____ are Russian.
3 Naomi and Hiroki are Japanese. _____ are from Tokyo.
4 My name's Klaus. _____ am from Germany.

2 Complete the sentences with the positive form of *be*. Use contractions.

I __'m__ Russian
1 We _____ French.
2 He _____ Spanish.
3 You _____ German.
4 She _____ from Egypt.

3 Make the sentences in exercise 2 negative.

I'm Russian – I'm not Russian

G **Grammar focus** – explanation & more practice of subject pronouns and *be* on page 106

Four students at the International School of English, London

I'm Chun Hei. I'm a student from Seoul in Korea. I'm not married.

My name's Elisaveta. I'm a student from Sofia in Bulgaria. I'm not married.

I'm Carola from Brazil. I'm a teacher in Rio de Janeiro. I'm married.

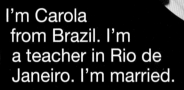

My name's Adriana. I'm a doctor from Milan, Italy. I'm married.

Reading and Listening

1 Look at the pictures and read about four language students in London.

2 ⏺ 1.21–1.23 Three of the women answer these questions. Listen and complete the table with Yes (Y) or No (N).

	1	2	3
Are you from Europe?	N		
Are you married?			
Are you a student?			

3 Read the text again. Write the names of women 1, 2 and 3.

Grammar

> *Are you married? Yes, **I am**.*
> *Are you students? No, **we aren't**.*

- start *yes / no* questions with the verb *be*
- do not use contractions for positive short answers (~~Yes, I'm~~ / ~~Yes, we're~~)

1 Complete the interview with Elisaveta.

Interviewer: Are _____ from Europe?
Elisaveta: Yes, _____ am.
Interviewer: _____ married?
Elisaveta: No, _____.
Interviewer: _____ a student?
Elisaveta: _____ am.

2 ⏺ 1.24 Listen again and check your answers.

Pronunciation and Speaking

1 ⏺ 1.25 Listen and repeat.
'Are you married?'   'Yes, I am.'
'Are you from Spain?'   'No, we aren't.'

2 Work in pairs. A: turn to page 96. B: turn to page 100. Ask and answer questions.

Functional language

1 Put the conversation in the correct order.
B: You too. Where are you from, Cem? ___
A: Hi. I'm Cem. _1_
A: Nice to meet you, Andrea. ___
A: I'm Turkish. I'm from Istanbul. And you? ___
B: I'm French. I'm from Paris. ___
B: Hi Cem, I'm Andrea. ___

2 ⏺ 1.26 Listen and check.

3 Work in pairs. Write a similar conversation about you.

A: Hi. I'm _____.
B: _____ .
A: _____.
B: _____. _____?
A: _____. _____. _____?
B: _____. _____.

4 Close your books. Practise the conversation with your partner.

Me & You

Part 2

Reading
Interview with Luis Ruiz

Listening
Asking questions

Grammar
Possessive adjectives (1)

Vocabulary
Numbers 11–20

Writing & Speaking
Personal details

Reading

1 Read *Interview with Luis Ruiz*. Complete the text with the answers from the box.

> Yes, it is. This is Rex.
> No, I'm not. I'm American.
> Yes, I am.
> I'm from Miami.

2 1.27 Listen and check.

Listening

1 1.28–1.31 Listen to the conversations 1–4 and match them to the pictures a–d.

2 Listen again and match the sentences to the conversations.

It's our dog. ___
Oh, they're my keys! ___
I'm Canadian. ___
Is this your car? ___

Interview with Luis Ruiz

Are you English, Luis?
_____

_____

Where are you from?
_____

_____

Are you a police officer?
_____

Is this your dog?
_____

a

b

c

d

Grammar

*I'm Canadian. They're **my** keys.*
*Where are **you** from? What's **your** name?*
*We're from Lyon. It's **our** dog.*

- *I / you / we* are subject pronouns
- use subject pronouns before the verb
- *my / your / our* are possessive adjectives
- use possessive adjectives before a noun

1 Change the subject pronouns to possessive adjectives.

This is (I) __my__ car.

1 A: 'What's (you) _____ postcode?'
   B: 'I don't know!'
2 This is (I) _____ address: 14 Wood Road.
3 We're on holiday. This is (we) _____ hotel.
4 A: 'Is this (you) _____ passport?'
   B: 'Yes, it is.'

2 Complete the sentences with possessive adjectives.

1 'What's _____ phone number, Mr Smith?' 'It's 329901.'
2 We're from Italy. _____ names are Lola and Silvio.
3 I'm Ronald. This is _____ car. It's a French car.
4 'We're the police. What's _____ nationality?' 'I'm French.'

3 🔊 1.32–1.33 Listen and check your answers to exercises 1 and 2.

ⓖ **Grammar focus** – explanation & more practice of possessive adjectives on page 106

Vocabulary

1 Complete the words with the letters *a e i o u*.

- **11** eleven
- **12** twelve
- **13** thirteen
- **14** f__rteen
- **15** f_fteen
- **16** s_xt__n
- **17** s_v_nt__n
- **18** __ght__n
- **19** n_n_t__n
- **20** twenty

2 🔊 1.34 Listen and repeat.

3 🔊 1.35–1.38 Listen and write the numbers you hear.

What's your address?	What's your postcode?
1 ___ Oxford Road.	L___ 3PQ
2 ___ King Street.	BS___ 5TW
3 ___ b London Road.	M___ 1A
4 ___ Park Street.	NW___ 4PT

Writing and Speaking

1 Look at picture a on page 14. Put the words in the correct order.

your Is car? this   *Is this your car?*
number? the What's   _____
name? your What's   _____
your What's address?   _____
from? are Where you   _____
you. OK, thank   _____

2 🔊 1.39 Listen and check.

3 Look at the picture again. Imagine you are in the car. Invent answers to the questions in exercise 1.

4 Work in pairs. Practise the conversation. Then swap roles and repeat.

Global voices

Warm up

Write the countries in the box next to the correct nationalities.

| France | Saudi Arabia | Scotland |
| Spain | United States | |

American   _____
Scottish   _____
French   _____
Saudi Arabian   _____
Spanish   _____

Listening

1 🎧 1.40–1.44 Listen to five people answering the questions *What's your name?* and *Where are you from?* Match the names to the places.

1 Pilar   France
2 Al-Mutasem   United States
3 Marc   Scotland
4 Dorothy   Spain
5 Mireille   Saudi Arabia

2 Listen again and underline the correct place.

1 Pilar   Barcelona / Sevilla / Madrid
2 Al-Mutasem   Riyadh / Jeddah / Dammam
3 Marc   Lyon / Paris / Marseille
4 Dorothy   Edinburgh / Glasgow / Alloa
5 Mireille   Los Angeles / Diamond Bar / San Diego

Language focus: question words

> **Language note:**
> use *what* to ask about things
> ***What's*** *your address?*
> use *where* to ask about places
> ***Where*** *are you from?*

Complete the questions.

1 _____'s your name?
2 _____ are you from?
3 _____'s your phone number?

Speaking

Ask four students the questions from the Language focus section and complete the table.

	name?	from?	phone number?
1			
2			
3			
4			

Pilar   Al-Mutasem   Marc   Dorothy   Mireille

Global review

Vocabulary

1 Complete the table.

Country	Nationality
Brazil	_____
_____	British
China	_____
_____	French
Japan	_____
_____	Polish
Portugal	_____
_____	Russian
Spain	_____
_____	American

2 Work with a partner. Look at the stamps. Where are they from?

3 1.45 Listen and check.

4 Write the missing numbers as words.

1 twelve, _____, fourteen
2 eighteen, _____, twenty
3 fourteen, _____, sixteen
4 seventeen, _____, nineteen

5 1.46 Write nine numbers from 11–20 in the table. Listen and cross out (✗) the numbers. When you have nine crosses, say *Bingo!*

Grammar

1 Circle the subject pronouns and <u>underline</u> the possessive adjectives.

> he I it my our she they
> we you <u>your</u>

2 Complete the description with the words in the box.

> are are he's He's is ~~My~~
> my Our She's

Hi. _My_ (1) name's Tina. This is _____ (2) English class. This is Gloria. _____ (3) from Argentina. The other students _____ (4) from Spain. This is Pedro. _____ (5) from Granada. And Carmen and Luis _____ (6) from Madrid. _____ (7) teacher's name _____ (8) Max and _____ (9) from Manchester.

3 1.47 Listen and check.

4 Write a description of your class.

Listen again

1 1.48 Listen again to the conversation from page 14. Cross out the words you do **not** hear.

A: Passport! Hello. What's your name, please?
B: My name's Smith, Jean Smith.
A: And where are you from Ms Smith?
B: I'm Canadian. I'm from Vancouver, British Columbia.
A: OK, thanks.
B: Thank you. Goodbye.

2 Match the words with the same meanings.

1 Hello   a Thank you
2 Thanks   b Bye
3 Goodbye   c Hi

Them & Us

Part 1

Reading & Vocabulary
1000 Families

Pronunciation
Linking words

Speaking
Describing a family

Grammar
Possessive adjectives (2)

Writing
Describing a family

These people are from *1000 families* by Uwe Ommer. This book has pictures of families from all over the world.

Reading and Vocabulary

1 Look at the pictures and read about three families from around the world. <u>Underline</u> the family words.

2 Are these family words male (M) or female (F)? Use the pictures to help you.

brother <u>M</u> ♂   sister <u>F</u> ♀
mother ___   father ___
husband ___   wife ___
daughter ___   son ___

3 🔘 1.49 Listen and repeat the words.

4 Read about the families again. Then read sentences 1–5. Which sentence is false?

1 Tahid and Hama are husband and wife.
2 Venus and Svetlana are children.
3 Svetlana and Olga are sisters.
4 Hama is a father.
5 Alla and Yakov are parents.

5 Work in pairs. What family words describe you? Tell your partner.

A: I'm a mother, wife and sister.

Pronunciation

🔘 1.50 Listen and repeat.

mother and father
son and daughter
husband and wife
brothers and sisters
parents and children

> **Language note:** some plural nouns are irregular.
> *One child, two* **children**
> *One person, two* **people**
> *One man, two* **men**
> *One woman, two* **women**

Speaking

Work in pairs. A: turn to page 96. B: turn to page 100. Describe a family.

Hama   Tahid   Venus

"Hi, I'm Svetlana. This is me and my family. This is Alla and Yakov. They're my <u>mother</u> and father. This is my sister, her name's Olga."

Svetlana Alla   Olga Yakov

Hong Suk   Palani

"Hello, I'm Tahid and this is my family. This is my wife, her name's Hama. This is my daughter, she's nine. Her name's Venus. This is my mother."

"Hello, my name's Hong Suk. This is my husband, his name's Palani. He's from Malaysia. This is my baby son."

Grammar

*He's from Malaysia. **His** name's Palani.*
*She's nine. **Her** name's Venus.*
*They're my mother and father. **Their** names are Alla and Yakov.*

- *he / she / they* are subject pronouns
- use subject pronouns before the verb
- *his / her / their* are possessive adjectives
- use possessive adjectives before a noun

| Sawaad | Lek | Arthit | Dao | Pichai |

1 Change the subject pronouns to possessive adjectives.

1 This is my brother and (he) ———— wife.
2 This is my sister and her husband, and (they) ———— children.
3 This is my mother and (she) ———— friend.

2 Complete the sentences with possessive adjectives.

1 My parents are from Iran. ———— names are Tahid and Hama.
2 Palani is from Malaysia and ———— wife is from Korea.
3 Svetlana is Russian. ———— family are from Gorodice.

3 Look at Flore and her family from France. Read the description and <u>underline</u> the correct words.

G **Grammar focus** – explanation & more practice of possessive adjectives on page 108

Writing

1 Work in pairs. Look at Dao and her family from Thailand. Match the names to the family words.

Sawaad	brother
Lek	father
Arthit	mother
Pichai	sister

Useful phrases

- I think Lek is her sister.
- Me too.
- Really? I think …

2 Write sentences about Dao and her family. Use the sentences about Flore to help you.

This is Dao, she's 12.

This is Flore, *her / she's* 11. *Her / She's* from France. This is *his / her* family. This is *his / her* father, *he / his* name's Thomas. This is *his / her* mother. This is her brother Didier, *his / he's* 6.

Them & Us

Part 2

Listening & Speaking
Family numbers

Vocabulary
Family

Grammar
Possession; Questions with be

Speaking
Your family

Reading and Listening
A family photograph

Functional language
Introducing people

Listening and Speaking

1 Read the information about families around the world.

 A typical family unit in South Africa is four people. In Sweden it's two. In Gambia a typical family has eight people.

2 🔊 1.51–1.55 Listen to five people. Write the numbers of people in their family.

1 Louise from Australia _4_
2 Sulayman from Gambia ___
3 Torsten from Germany ___
4 Noriko from Japan ___
5 Hasna from Morocco ___

Language note: use *How many* to ask about numbers.
How many people are in your family?

3 Ask other students in the class about the number of people in their family.

A: *How many people are in your family?*
B: *Six. And you?*

Vocabulary

1 🔊 1.56 Listen again to Hasna. (Circle) the words you hear.

brother	daughter	father	husband
mother	niece	sister	son	wife

2 🔊 1.57 Listen and repeat the words in the family tree.

Grammar

my sister's daughter
my husband's family

* use *'s* to talk about possession

1 Match the descriptions to the family words.

1 my mother's mother ⎫ my aunt
2 my father's sister ⎪ my brother-in-law
3 my sister's husband ⎬ my cousin
4 my sister's son ⎪ my grandmother
5 my aunt's daughter ⎭ my nephew

2 Write a definition (or definitions) for these family words.

my niece = my brother's daughter / my sister's daughter

1 my sister-in-law
2 my grandfather
3 my uncle
4 my mother-in-law
5 my nephew

G **Grammar focus –** explanation & more practice of possession on page 108

Speaking

Write the names of four people in your family. Work in pairs. Ask questions about your partner's names.

A: *Who's Jochen?*
B: *He's my grandfather.*
A: *Who's Christine?*
B: *She's my brother's wife.*

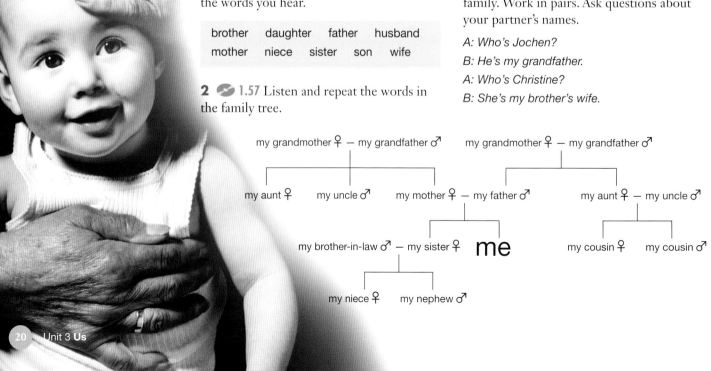

my grandmother ♀ — my grandfather ♂   my grandmother ♀ — my grandfather ♂

my aunt ♀   my uncle ♂   my mother ♀ — my father ♂   my aunt ♀ — my uncle ♂

my brother-in-law ♂ — my sister ♀   **me**   my cousin ♀   my cousin ♂

my niece ♀   my nephew ♂

Me **Christopher**

A: This is my family at my sister's birthday party in London. This is me and this is my brother James.
B: OK - is he married?
A: Yes, he is. His wife isn't in the photo. She's in Australia.
B: Oh right. Is she Australian?
A: No she isn't. She's English. She's a student in Sydney.
B: And who's this?
A: Oh, that's Christopher, my other brother. And that's Lucy.
B: Are they married?
A: No, they aren't. Christopher's single and Lucy's our cousin.

Reading and Listening

1 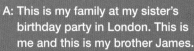 1.58 Read and listen to a conversation about the picture. Write the names *James* (♂) and *Lucy* (♀) next to the people in the photo.

2 Are the sentences true (T) or false (F)?

1 James is in Sydney. ___
2 James is married. ___
3 Christopher is in London. ___
4 Christopher is James's brother ___
5 Lucy is Christopher's wife. ___

Grammar

Is he married? Yes, **he is.**
Are they married? No, **they aren't**

- start yes/no questions with the verb *be*
- do not use contractions for positive short answers (~~Yes, she's~~ / ~~Yes, they're~~)

1 Put the words in the correct order to make questions.

Christopher / is / in Sydney?

Is Christopher in Sydney?

1 at a party? / the family / is
2 James / in London? / is
3 in Sydney? / James and Lucy / are
4 Lucy / married? / are / Christopher / and

2 Write short answers to the questions in exercise 1.

Is Christopher in Sydney? No, he isn't.

3 Read the conversation about this photograph. <u>Underline</u> the correct words.

A: OK. So who's this?
B: That's my sister Clare and her husband Jed.
A: *Jed is / Is Jed* English?
B: No, *he isn't / he not*. He's Irish.
A: And *are this / is this* their daughter?
B: No, that's our cousin Danielle.
A: *Are / Are they* here in Manchester?
B: No, they *aren't / isn't*. They're in Dublin.

4 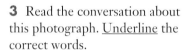 1.59 Listen and check.

(G) **Grammar focus** – explanation & more practice of questions with *be* on page 108

Functional language

1 Complete the conversations with the words in the box.

brother   from   Hi   is   you

1 A: Juliet, this _____ Nigel. He's _____ Canada.
  B: Hello Nigel. Nice to meet _____.

2 A: Naomi, this is my _____ Lee.
  B: _____ Lee.

2 1.60 Listen and check.

3 Work in pairs. Practise the conversations.

4 Introduce your partner to other students in the class.

Global reading

1 Look at this information about Isabella Cerase. Where is it from?

a A newspaper   b A magazine

c A website   d A book

Isabella Cerase

About me

Hi! My name's Isabella. I'm 24. I'm Italian, I'm from Rome. Now I'm in London with my brothers and a friend.

Isabella's friends

Maria Fernández, Spain	Maria is with her family.
Maciej Królak, Poland	Maciej is 19 today!
Eva Emillina, Italy	Eva is in Milan.
Luigi Cerase, Italy	Luigi is in Oxford Street, London.
Brigitte Bouzain, France	Brigitte is at a birthday party.
Paolo Cerase, Italy	Paulo is with Isabella in England.
Ana Pérez, Spain	Ana is in a café.
Sandra Brown, UK	Sandra is with Isabella!
Gianpiero Todaro, Italy	Gianpiero is with his uncle.

2 Read the information. Are the sentences true (T) or false (F)?

1 Isabella is from Italy. _T_
2 She's from Milan. ___
3 Her brothers' names are Luigi and Gianpiero. ___
4 She's in Rome. ___
5 Maciej is Polish. ___
6 Sandra is in London with three people. ___
7 Four friends are with family members. ___

3 Look at the *About me* paragraph. Write a true paragraph about you.

Hi! My name's…

Global review

Vocabulary

1 Write three more words in each group.

female family members	male family members	*grand*
mother	son	grandmother
aunt	husband	grandchildren
_____	_____	_____
_____	_____	_____
_____	_____	_____

2 Work in pairs. What is the answer to this question?

'This person is my father's son but he's not my brother. Who is it?'

a my uncle   b my sister   c me

Grammar

1 <u>Underline</u> the correct word.

1 *I / My* am married.
2 *I / My* sister's name is Jill.
3 *She / Her* husband's name is Andy.
4 *He / His* is from Jamaica.
5 *They / Their* children are ten and six.

2 Write five sentences about your family. Write four true sentences and one false sentence. Work in pairs. Read your sentences to your partner. Your partner guesses which sentence is false.

Listen again

1 🎧 1.61 Read and listen to the conversation from page 21. Who do the words in **bold** refer to?

1 *he* = James
A: This is my family at my sister's birthday party in London. This is me and this is my brother James.
B: OK – is (1) **he** married?
A: Yes, he is. (2) **His** wife isn't in the photo. She's in Australia.
B: Oh right. Is she Australian?
A: No she isn't. She's English. (3) **She**'s a student in Sydney.
B: And who's this?
A: Oh, that's Christopher, my other brother. And that's Lucy.
B: Are (4) **they** married?
A: No, they aren't. Christopher's single and Lucy's our cousin.

2 Read the second conversation from page 21. Replace the words in **bold** with *he*, *our*, *they* or *their*.

A: OK. So who's this?
B: That's my sister Clare and her husband Jed.
A: Is Jed English?
B: No, **Jed** isn't. **Jed**'s Irish.
A: And is this **Jed and Clare**'s daughter?
B: No, that's **my and Clare**'s cousin Danielle.
A: Are **Jed, Clare and Danielle** here in Manchester?
B: No, they aren't. They're in Dublin.

3 🎧 1.62 Listen and check.

Big & Small

Part 1

Vocabulary
Numbers 20–100

Vocabulary & Reading
Shopping in numbers

Grammar
There is / There are

Pronunciation & Speaking
schwa /ə/

Writing
Describing a hotel

Vocabulary

1 Write the words in the box with the numbers.

sixty	forty	ninety	seventy	
eighty	thirty	~~twenty~~	fifty	hundred

20 _twenty_   **70** _____
30 _____   **80** _____
40 _____   **90** _____
50 _____   **100** _____
60 _____

2 🔊 1.63 Listen, check and repeat.

3 Write the words for the numbers.

50 _fifty_   7 _seven_ → 57 _fifty-seven_
30 _____   9 _____ → 39 _____
60 _____   1 _____ → 61 _____
24 _____
82 _____
33 _____

4 Match the numbers with the words.

23   forty-six
46   ninety-eight
89   sixty-four
32   eighty-nine
64   thirty-two
98   twenty-three

5 🔊 1.64 Listen and write the numbers you hear as words.

1 _forty-two_   3 _____
2 _____   4 _____

Vocabulary and Reading

1 🔊 1.65 Look at the pictures of places in a town. Listen and repeat the words.

2 Is there a big shopping mall in your town?

3 Read about a shopping mall on page 25. Complete the text with the numbers.

Language note:

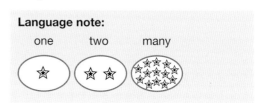

one   two   many

4 🔊 1.66 Listen and check.

a supermarket

b restaurant   c car park   d shopping mall   e cinema   f shop

Grammar

> **There's** a big supermarket.
> **There are** 48 restaurants.
> **Is there** a cinema?
> **Are there** any banks?
> > Yes, there are.
> > No, there aren't.

- use *There's* (*There is*) with singular nouns
- use *There are* with plural nouns
- start questions with *Is there …?* or *Are there …?*
- use *any* after *Are there …?*

1 Read the sentences about a shopping mall. Decide which four sentences are incorrect. Then correct them.

There's four restaurants. ✗

There are four restaurants. ✔

1 There's two floors.
2 There are one cinema.
3 There's six floors for shopping.
4 There is a big car park for eighty cars.
5 There are two supermarkets.
6 There's many people.

2 Underline the correct words.

1 *Is there / Are there* any restaurants?
2 *Is there / Are there* a bank?
3 *Is there / Are there* a supermarket?
4 *Is there / Are there* a car park?
5 *Is there / Are there* any cinemas?

G **Grammar focus** – explanation & more practice of *there is* and *there are* on page 108

Pronunciation and Speaking

1 🔊 1.67 Listen to how the <u>underlined</u> sound is pronounced. Repeat the sentences.

1 There's <u>a</u> cin<u>e</u>ma.
2 Is there <u>a</u> bank?
3 It's busy on Sat<u>u</u>rday.

2 Work in pairs. A: turn to page 96. B: turn to page 100. Talk about two other shopping malls.

Shopping in Numbers

There are shopping malls everywhere from **A**lgeria to **Z**ambia but they're not just for shopping.

48
restaurants
cinemas **4** shops

'In this mall there are _____ floors for shopping and a big car park with _____ floors for cars. There are many interesting shops and there's a big supermarket. But it's not just for shopping: there are _____ restaurants and a cinema with _____ screens.'

floors **6** screens
supermarkets **11**

Cevahir shopping mall, Istanbul, Turkey

Writing

1 Look at this information about the Allstar Hotel. Write some sentences. Use the text about the shopping mall to help you.

- 20 floors
- 4 restaurants
- 2 cafés
- 25 shops
- one bank
- one big car park for 60 cars

In the Allstar Hotel there are twenty floors …

Big & Small

Part 2

Vocabulary & Speaking

Prices

Functional language

In a shop

Reading & Vocabulary

A small shop near my house; adjectives

Writing & Speaking

A shop near your house

Vocabulary and Speaking

1 🔊 1.68 Listen and repeat the prices.

$4.50   £39   €10.99   £75.42 $25

> **Language note:** $ = dollar, £ = pound, €= euro

2 🔊 1.69 Listen to the conversations and ⟨circle⟩ the price you hear.

1	a £24	b £42	c £25
2	a $19	b $90	c $99
3	a €13.30	b €3.30	c €1.30
4	a £7.49	b £6.49	c £6.90

3 Write four prices. Work in pairs. Say the prices to your partner. Your partner writes the prices. Then swap roles and repeat.

4 Work in pairs. Look at the pictures and prices. Ask and answer with a partner.

A: How much is the cola?

B: It's $1.

5 Compare the prices with your country. Are they cheap, expensive or the same?

A: The magazine is $3.00. In my country that's about 39 pesos. That's expensive!

B: Oh, for me it's cheap.

Functional language

1 Complete the conversation with the words in the box.

Thank you	Bye	How much is	Hello

Shop Assistant: _____.
Customer: Hi. _____ the magazine?
Shop Assistant: $3.00, please.
Customer: Here you are. Thanks.
Shop Assistant: _____. Goodbye.
Customer: _____.

2 🔊 1.70 Listen and check.

3 Work in pairs. Practise the conversation.

4 Work in pairs. Look at the pictures and prices again. Make a similar conversation.

Useful phrases

- How much is ... ?
- Here you are.
- Thank you.

cola $1   milk $1.38   bread $1.97

newspaper $1.25   magazine $3.00

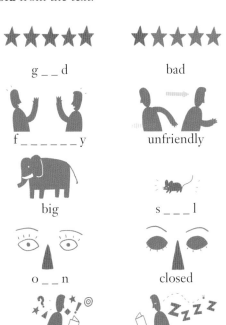

A small shop near my house

> **1**
> 'There's a bakery near my house. The bread is very **good** and the people are **friendly**.'

> **2**
> 'The shop near my house is very **small** but there are lots of things to buy. It's **open** 17 hours a day from 6.00am to 11.00pm.'

> **3**
> '*Bob's News* is a **small** shop in my street. There are lots of newspapers and magazines. There are other things too – Coke®, milk and chocolate.'

> **4**
> 'There's a **small** bookshop near my house. There are many **interesting**, **old** books in the shop. It isn't an **expensive** shop, the books are **cheap**.'

Reading and Vocabulary

1 🔊 1.71–1.74 Read and listen to four people talking about a shop near their house. Match 1–4 to the pictures a–d.

2 Look at the pairs of opposite adjectives. Complete the words with the adjectives in **bold** from the text.

★★★★★ g _ _ d   ★★★★★ bad

f _ _ _ _ _ y   unfriendly

big   s _ _ _ l

o _ _ n   closed

i _ _ _ _ _ _ _ g   boring

o _ d   new

c _ _ p   e _ _ _ _ _ _ e

3 🔊 1.75 Listen, check and repeat.

4 Underline the adjectives you can use to describe the nouns.

city: *big closed old*
1 student: good friendly expensive
2 café: open small unfriendly
3 book: boring closed new
4 holiday: boring cheap closed
5 grandfather: old expensive interesting

Writing and Speaking

1 Think about a small shop near your house. Make some notes.

name of the shop: _____
adjectives to describe the shop: _____

2 Write a short description about the shop. Use the descriptions about the four shops to help you.

3 Work in small groups. Tell the other students about your shop.

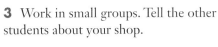

Global game

1 Work in pairs. Look at the picture and say what you can see. How many sentences can you say?

There is a cinema.

The camera is £89.

2 🔊 **1.76** Work in pairs. Listen and answer the questions.

Global review

c _i_ _n_ _e_ _m_ _a_

b _ _ _

r _ _ _ _ _ _ _ _ _

h _ _ _ _

Vocabulary

1 Write the name of the places under the pictures.

2 Write eight more numbers in the table. Work in pairs and read the numbers to your partner.

63								

3 Listen and write your partner's numbers here.

63								

4 Work in pairs. Say a number from 11 to 99. Your partner says the opposite.

A: 23   B: 32

A: 45   B: 54

5 Put the tiles in the correct order to make adjectives.

L	AL	SM

SM	AL	L

1 | OS | ED | CL |

2 | EA | P | CH |

3 | PE | IV | NS | E | EX |

4 | IE | LY | FR | ND |

5 | TE | I | NG | IN | RE | ST |

Grammar

Tick (✔) the correct sentence or question.

a   There's a shopping mall. ✔
b   There a shopping mall.

1 a   There are 85 shops in the mall.
   b   There's 85 shops in the mall.
2 a   There's many people shopping on Saturdays.
   b   There are many people shopping on Saturdays.
3 a   Is there two or three bookshops?
   b   Are there two or three bookshops?
4 a   Is there a car park?
   b   Are there a car park?

Listen again

1 💿 1.77–1.80 Listen to the speakers from page 27. Complete the sentences with the adjectives in the box.

expensive   friendly   good   interesting   open   small

1   There's a bakery near my house. The bread is very _____ and the people are _____ .
2   The shop near my house is very small but there are lots of things to buy. It's _____ 17 hours a day from 6.00am to 11.00pm.
3   *Bob's News* is a _____ shop in my street. There are lots of newspapers and magazines. There are other things too – Coke®, milk and chocolate.
4   There's a small bookshop near my house. There are many _____, old books in the shop. It isn't an _____ shop, the books are cheap.

2 Listen again and check.

3 Look at *A small shop near my house* again on page 27. Choose one of the speakers and practise reading what they say.

Work & Play

Part 1

Reading
VSO

Grammar
There isn't / There aren't

Listening
Describing jobs

Vocabulary & Speaking
Jobs

Reading

1 Read the introduction to the text about VSO in the information box on page 31. Then look at the pictures of VSO volunteers and complete the sentences with the words in the box.

school	farm	hospital

2 🔊 2.01 Listen and read more about VSO. Choose the best title for the text.
- VSO – an International Organisation
- Working for VSO
- The History of VSO

3 Are the following sentences true (T) or false (F)?
1 VSO is an American organisation. ___
2 Many volunteers work in Africa and Asia. ___
3 There are volunteers in North Africa. ___
4 Guyana is a South Asian country. ___
5 There isn't a lot of time for fun. ___

4 Do you think working for VSO is interesting? Why?

Yes, because …
No, because …

Grammar

There isn't *a lot of money for volunteers.*
There aren't *any volunteers in North Africa.*

- use *there isn't* with singular nouns
- use *there aren't* with plural nouns
- use *any* after *there aren't*

1 Underline the correct words.
1 There *isn't / aren't* any volunteers in Brazil.
2 There *isn't / aren't* a VSO office in Egypt.
3 There *isn't / aren't* any volunteers who are seventeen years old.
4 There *isn't / aren't* any volunteers on farms.

2 Complete the sentences with *There isn't* or *There aren't*.
1 _____ any volunteers in my country.
2 _____ a teacher in the classroom.
3 _____ any friendly students here.
4 _____ a school café for the students.

3 Are the sentences in exercise 2 true or false for you?

G **Grammar focus** – explanation & more practice of *there isn't* and *there aren't* on page 110

Listening

1 🔊 2.02–2.07 Listen to six people talking about their jobs. How many people work for VSO?

2 Listen again and match the names to the sentences.

Jim — I work outdoors, it's *easy / difficult*.
David ⟩ I work in a hospital, it's *quiet / busy*.
Ingrid ⟍ I work in a shop, it's *boring / interesting*.
Maria I work in an office, the people are *friendly / unfriendly*.
Richard I work in a restaurant, it's *quiet / busy*.
Julie I work in a school, it's *boring / interesting*.

3 Listen again and underline the correct words.

Language note: use *I work...* to talk about your job.
*I **work** in a restaurant / outdoors.*

Vocabulary and Speaking

1 Turn to page 104 and match the jobs to the pictures.

2 Look at the table. Choose **one** of the tasks below.

A Tick (✔) the sentence which is true for you.

B Choose a job from page 104. This is your job. Tick (✔) the true sentence.

		you
I work ...	in a school.	
	in an office.	
	in a shop.	
	in a restaurant.	
	outdoors.	
	at home.	
	...	
I'm a student.		
I'm unemployed.		
I'm retired.		

Language note: someone who is **unemployed** does not have a job. Someone who is **retired** does not have a job because they are over 60 or 65 years old.

3 Speak to five other people in the class and make a note of their answers.

A: *I work in a shop. And you?*
B: *I'm a student.*

4 Are these sentences true (T) or false (F)?

In my group ...
• three people work in an office. ___
• two people are unemployed. ___
• one person is a student. ___
• nobody is retired. ___

VSO is a British organisation; it works with people in many countries. VSO workers are called *volunteers*.

VSO
Sharing skills
Changing lives

There are 1,500 VSO volunteers and they work in over 40 countries. There are many volunteers in Asian countries including China, India and Indonesia. There are also many volunteers in African countries but there aren't any volunteers in North Africa. Volunteers also work in South America in Guyana, Bolivia and Peru.

Volunteers are from 18 to 75 years old; the average age of a volunteer is 42. Most volunteers work for two years. They work in many different places including schools, hospitals, offices and outdoors on farms.

There isn't a lot of money for volunteers – only for food and a house. There's a lot of work but there's time for fun too.

A volunteer in a _____ in Malawi.

A VSO volunteer in a _____ in Guyana.

A volunteer on a _____ in Kenya.

Work & Play

Part 2

Vocabulary & Speaking
Sports

Listening
Talking about sports

Grammar & Pronunciation
Like

Reading & Speaking
The Human Race

Vocabulary and Speaking

1 Write the missing vowels (*a, e, i, o, u*) to complete the names of the sports.

2 ⏺ 2.08 Listen and repeat the sports.

3 Work in pairs. Look at the bar chart of countries and their national sports. Guess the sports. Choose from the sports in exercise 1.

A: I think number one is swimming. What do you think?

B: I think it's basketball.

4 ⏺ 2.09 Listen and check.

5 Work in pairs. Ask and answer the questions.

- Which sports are popular in your country?
- Which sports are *not* popular?
- Is there a national sport?

Listening

1 Do you like the sports in Vocabulary and Speaking exercise 1? Write **+++** (I love it), **++** (I like it), **+** (it's OK) or **x** (I don't like it) in the boxes.

2 ⏺ 2.10 Listen to two people talking about some sports. Tick (✔) the table.

		+++ I love it	**++** I like it	**+** It's OK	**x** I don't like it
football	Man				
	Woman		✔		
swimming	Man				
	Woman				

3 Listen again and put the conversation in the correct order.

No, I don't. ___

Really? I love it. ___

Do you like football? _1_

Well, it's OK. ___

What about swimming, Steve? Do you like swimming? ___

Yes, I do. And you? ___

National sports of the world

Bar chart:
1 — Brazil, Cameroon, Russia, England, Sudan, Poland
2 — India, Australia, Pakistan, Jamaica
3 — US, Canada
4 — China

sw__mm__ng

r__nn__ng

t__bl__ t__nn__s

cr__ck__t

b__sk__tb__ll

__m__r__c__n f__tb__ll

f__tb__ll

Grammar and Pronunciation

Do you like football?
Yes, **I do**. */ No,* **I don't**.

- start questions with the auxiliary verb *do*
- use *do* for short answers, **not** the main verb (*Yes, I like*)

1 <u>Underline</u> the correct words.

A: Do you *like / likes* basketball?

B: Yes, I *do / don't*. It's a very popular sport in my country. In Argentina we love all ball sports – football, tennis, basketball. *Like you / Do you like* basketball?

A: No, *I don't / I don't like*. It's boring. *I do like / I like* running.

2 Write words to complete the questions.

Do you like <u>tennis</u> *(a sport)?*

1 Do you like _____ (a sport)?
2 Do you like _____ (a sportsman or sportswoman)?
3 Do you like _____ (a nationality) restaurants?
4 Do you like _____ (an actor)?

3 Write your answers to the questions.

Do you like tennis?   No, I don't.

4 🔊 **2.11** Read and listen to these sentences from the Listening on page 32. Notice how the words connect.

Do‿you like football?
Yes,‿I do.
Do‿you like swimming?
No,‿I don't.

5 Listen again and repeat.

6 Work in pairs. Ask and answer questions 1–4 from exercise 2. Remember to connect the words. Use short answers.

A: Do you like tennis?

B: Yes, I do.

G **Grammar focus –** explanation & more practice of *like* on page 110

- The Human Race
- 10 kilometres
- 1 million runners worldwide
- Races in many cities (including London, Istanbul, Lima, Taipei, Warsaw ...) or run where you live

Reading and Speaking

1 Work in pairs. Do you like running? Ask your partner.

2 Look at the picture of a race and read the information. Then answer the questions.

1 What's the name of the race?
2 Where is it?
3 How many kilometres is the race?
4 What's special about this race?

3 Work in pairs. A: turn to page 97. B: turn to page 101. Tell your partner about another race.

4 Work in pairs. Are there any important races in your town or country? Tell your partner.

Global voices

capoeira

ski-jumping

dancing

judo

motorbike racing

Warm up

1 🔊 **2.12** Listen and repeat the names of the sports in the pictures.

2 Look at the sports in the box.

> basketball   capoeira   dancing   football   golf
> judo   motorbike racing   running   ski-jumping
> swimming   tennis

Find sports you ...
- play with a ball.
- normally do indoors.
- normally do with one other person.
- normally do alone.

Listening

1 🔊 **2.13–2.17** Listen to five people answer the questions *Do you like sport?* and *What's your favourite sport?* Write the speaker's number next to the phrases.

a Not football. ___
b Well, I mean, yes, quite a bit. Not too much, but yes. ___
c I do like sport, but not too much. ___
d Yes, I do. ___
e I love sports. _1_

2 Listen again and write the speakers' favourite sports from the list in Warm up exercise 2.

1 Mireille, US _____
2 Christina, Germany _____
3 Francesco, Italy _____
4 Jolanta, Poland _____
5 Eva, Switzerland _____

Language focus: questions

> **Language note:** for questions starting with *do* we normally give *Yes / No* answers. For *Wh-* questions (*Where*, *What* etc) we give information in the answer.
> *Do you like sport?   Yes, I do.*
> *What's your favourite sport?   My favourite sport is golf.*

<u>Underline</u> the correct answer for each question.

1 A: Do you like sport?
   B: *My favourite? Cricket. / Yes, it's OK.*
2 A: What's your favourite type of music?
   B: *I love it. / Opera – I love opera.*
3 A: Do you like the cinema?
   B: *Well, yes, but not too much. / I like Titanic.*
4 A: What's your favourite food?
   B: *No, I don't. / Chinese food.*
5 A: Do you like Italian restaurants?
   B: *Yes, I do, they're great. / My favourite is pizza.*

Speaking

Work in pairs. Ask and answer the questions from the Language focus section.

Global review

Vocabulary

1 Write six places where people work in the crossword puzzle. Use the pictures to help you.

r	e	s	t	a	u	r	a	n	t
		c							
		h							
		o							
		o							
		l							

2 Complete the words.

A person over 65 who doesn't work is _r _ _ _ _ _._

A person who doesn't have a job is _u _ _ _ _ _ _ _ _._

3 Put the letters in the correct order to spell six sports.

1 laebsbktal   4 tckrcie
2 snetin   5 nsimgiwm
3 folatobl   6 nungirn

Grammar

1 Read a teacher's description of her school. Complete the sentences with *there's*, *there are*, *there isn't* or *there aren't*.

'I work in a school, it's a small school. _____ one head teacher and _____ 5 teachers. It's a school for girls. _____ 80 girls in the school. The girls are from 5 to 11 years old. _____ any boys. I like my job, _____ a boring day – every day is busy and interesting!'

2 Look at the table. Write five more sentences.

		+++ I love it	++ I like it	+ It's OK	x I don't like it
tennis	I	✔			
	You		✔		
swimming	I			✔	
	You			✔	
cricket	I				✔
	You	✔			
football	I		✔		
	You				✔

1 I love tennis.   5 You like tennis.
2 I think swimming is OK.   6 You _____.
3 _____ cricket.   7 _____.
4 _____.   8 _____.

3 Underline the correct answer.

1 Do you like tennis?   Yes, I *like / do*.
2 Do you like cricket?   Yes, *I love it / I do like*.
3 Do you like swimming?   *Is OK / It's OK*.
4 Do you like football?   No, *I don't / not like*.

Writing

1 Complete the sentences with information about yourself.

Hello, my name's _____, I'm from _____.
I work _____. I'm _____.
In my country the national sport is _____.
I like _____ but I don't like _____.

Listen again

1 2.18 Read and listen to these sentences from the Listening on page 30. Notice how the words link together.

I work in a shop, it's a small shop.
It's open every day.
It's OK, but it's a bit boring.

2 Repeat the sentences. Remember to link the words.

3 Read these phrases from the listening and decide which words link together.

I work outdoors on a farm.
It's a good job, but it's a difficult job too.

4 2.19 Listen and check. Repeat the sentences.

Day & Night

Part 1

Functional language
Telling the time

Listening & Vocabulary
Daily routine / have and go

Reading
A day in my life

Grammar
Present simple

Writing
A day in the life of ...

Functional language

1 Match the times to the clocks.

1 six twenty   `11:30`

2 five thirty-five   `07:05`

3 eleven thirty   `05:35`

4 three o'clock   `04:45`

5 seven oh-five   `03:00`

6 four forty-five   `06:20`

2 🔊 2.20–2.23 Listen and write the times you hear.

1 _____   3 _____

2 _____   4 _____

3 🔊 2.24 Listen again to number 4. Put the lines in the correct order.

B: Let's see – it's two thirty. ___
A: OK. Thank you. ___
A: Excuse me. What's the time? _1_
A: Sorry? ___
B: Two thirty. ___

4 Work in pairs. Practise similar conversations.

Listening and Vocabulary

1 🔊 2.25 Look at the pictures and times. Listen and tick (✔) the correct times.

2 Listen again and correct the incorrect times.

3 Listen again and complete the expressions with *have* or *go*.

1	_____ a shower	5	_____ to the gym
2	_____ breakfast	6	_____ home
3	_____ to work	7	_____ dinner
4	_____ lunch	8	_____ to bed

Language note: use *at* to talk about time.
Use *at about* when a time is not exact.
I go to work **at** 7.
I go to work **at about** 7. (6.50–7.10)

4 What time do you do the things in exercise 3? Write some sentences.

I have a shower at 7.30.

5 🔊 2.26 Listen and repeat the conversation.

A: What time do you have breakfast?
B: At about 8.00.

6 Work in pairs. Ask your partner *What time do you ...?* Write your partner's answers.

A: What time do you have a shower?
B: At 7.30.
shower – 7.30

7.00 ☐   7.20 ☐   8.00 ☐   1.00 ☐

6.30 ☐   7.45 ☐   8.30 ☐   11.30 ☐

Nelson

A day in my life

Nelson is an engineer in Malawi.
Linda is an office worker in England.
Read about a typical day in their lives.

Nelson is an engineer. He works in an office in Lilongwe, the capital of Malawi. His day starts early – he has breakfast at about five thirty. He goes to work at seven o'clock **and** starts work at seven thirty. He has lunch at twelve thirty **and** goes home at five o'clock. **After that** he has dinner – at about six o'clock. He watches television and goes to bed at ten o'clock.

Linda works in an office in Leeds, England. She has breakfast with her husband and children at seven thirty **and** goes to work at eight fifteen. She starts work at nine o'clock. She has lunch at twelve thirty. She finishes work at three thirty **and then** she goes to her children's school. **After that** they go home – at about four fifteen. They have dinner at six o'clock. Linda and her husband go to bed at eleven thirty.

Linda

Reading

1 Work in pairs. Read the introduction to *A day in my life*. Student A, read about Nelson. Student B, read about Linda. Then complete the times in the table for Nelson or Linda.

He / she …	Nelson	Linda
has / goes breakfast at	5.30	
has / goes to work at		
has / goes lunch at		
has / goes home at		
has / goes dinner at		
has / goes to bed at		

2 Underline the correct word *has* or *goes* for each phrase in the table.

3 Work in pairs. Tell your partner about Nelson or Linda. Listen to your partner and complete the table. What's the same? What's different?

A: Nelson has breakfast at 5.30 – and Linda?
B: Linda has breakfast at 7.30. That's different.

Grammar

> I **have** a shower at 7.00.
> He **watches** television.
> She **starts** work at 9.00.

- we use the present simple to say what we do every day
- after *I / you / we / they* the verb form is usually the same as the infinitive
- after *he / she / it* the verb usually ends in *-s* or *-es*

1 Write the correct form of the verb.

She _goes_ (go) to work at 8.30.
1 I _____ (have) a shower at 8.00.
2 He _____ (work) in a hospital.
3 You _____ (start) work at 9.30.
4 She _____ (have) a coffee at work.
5 We _____ (finish) lunch at 1.30.
6 The class _____ (start) at 7.30.
7 They _____ (go) home at 5.45.

2 Look at your notes from Listening and Vocabulary exercise 6. Write some sentences about your partner.

lunch – 12.30   Tito has lunch at 12.30.

G **Grammar focus** – explanation & more practice of present simple on page 110

Writing

1 Look at the words in **bold** in the texts about Nelson and Linda.

> **Language note:** use *and* to connect two ideas. Use *then* or *after that* to say what happens next.
> *He goes to work at 7.00 **and** starts at 7.30.*
> *She finishes work at 3.30 **and then** she goes to her children's school.*

2 Think of a friend or someone in your family. Write about a typical day in their life. Use *and*, *then* and *after that*.

3 Work in pairs. Compare your description with your partner's. Is it the same or different?

Day & Night

Part 2

Vocabulary & Pronunciation
The time, word stress

Speaking & Vocabulary
Your favourite time of day

Reading & Listening
24/7 Services

Grammar
Present simple negative

Functional language
Giving an opinion

Vocabulary and Pronunciation

1 Look at the diagram showing another way of telling the time. Then tick (✔) the correct times below.

 1 half past two ✔

 2 a quarter past six ✗

3 five to eight

4 four o'clock

5 a quarter to nine

6 two o'clock

7 ten past ten

8 ten to eleven

2 Correct the incorrect times in exercise 1.

2 – *a quarter to seven*

3 🔊 **2.27** Listen and repeat the correct times in exercise 1. Listen for the stress.

1 *half past two*

4 Work in pairs. A: say a time. B: say the same time differently.

A: It's a quarter past two.
B: It's two fifteen.

Speaking and Vocabulary

1 Look at the pictures. What times are morning, afternoon, evening and night for you? Work in pairs. Compare your ideas with your partner.

For me morning is 4.00am to 12.00pm.
Really? For me morning is…

> **Language note:** *am* means in the morning, *pm* means in the afternoon or evening
> *I get up at 7.00**am**. I go to bed at 11.00**pm**.*

2 Work in groups. What's your favourite time of day? Tell your group.

My favourite time of the day is the morning, at about six o'clock.

Extend your Vocabulary – good + time of day

Use *good morning / afternoon/ evening* to say hello to someone politely.
Use *goodnight* to say goodbye to someone before you go to bed.

Complete the sentences with *good morning*, *good afternoon*, *good evening* or *goodnight*.

1 _____. It's 3.00pm and this is the BBC news.
2 I'm very tired, it's time for bed. _____.
3 _____! Tea or coffee for breakfast?
4 _____ sir – here's your table for dinner.

morning afternoon evening night

Reading and Listening

1 Complete the sentence with the words in the box.

day   days   hours   week

24/7 means 24 _____ a _____, 7 _____ a _____.

2 Read the text about 24/7 services. Find …
- three jobs.
- three places where people work.
- three expressions that mean 24/7.

3 🔊 2.28–2.31 Look at the pictures and listen to four people talking about 24/7 services. Number the pictures in the order you hear them.

Grammar

> *A taxi driver* **doesn't have** *a nine to five job.*
> *People* **don't have** *time to shop.*
> *I* **don't have** *time to phone in the day.*

- use *don't* or *doesn't* before the verb to make the present simple negative
- use *don't* (do not) after *I / you / we / they*
- use *doesn't* (does not) after *he / she / it*
- use the infinitive form of the main verb (*have, work*, etc)

1 Complete the sentences from Reading and Listening exercise 3 with the negative form of the verb.

I _don't have_ *(have) time to phone in the day and at night it isn't so expensive.*

1 My wife _____ (like) it because I work all night.
2 I _____ (work) normal hours.
3 I like my job, but we _____ (have) time to see other people.
4 My supermarket _____ (close) at night.
5 You _____ (spend) hours in the shop.

2 🔊 2.32 Listen and check.

3 Write some sentences about you. Use positive and negative forms of the verb.

4 Work in pairs. Read your sentences to your partner.

ⓖ **Grammar focus** – explanation & more practice of present simple negative on page 110

Functional language

1 🔊 2.33 Listen again to speaker 4 from Reading and Listening exercise 3. Write the missing word.

24 hour shopping? I think it's _____.

2 Look at more words we use to give an opinion. Match them to the symbols.

bad   fantastic   good   ~~great~~
OK   terrible

I think it's …
+++ _great_ _____
++ _____
+ _____
x _____
x x _____

3 Work in pairs. A: turn to page 97. B: turn to page 101. Give your opinion on working and shopping.

24/7 Services

Round the clock care

Hospitals are open all day, every day. Doctors, nurses and other hospital workers don't stop at night.

Shop when you want

Many supermarkets now open 24/7. People don't have time to shop in the day. They come at night.

Taxi!

A taxi driver doesn't have a nine to five job. People use taxis at all hours, day and night.

Service night and day

People phone call centres at all hours. Call centres don't close at night.

Global reading

1 Look at this page from a website. Choose the best way to complete each sentence.

1 People use this website …
 a to write to friends.
 b to get answers to a question.

2 The people who answer are …
 a normal people.
 b experts.

2 Read Jan's question and the answers. Who has a good answer? Complete the answer ratings. Use one to five stars (⭐).

3 Work in pairs. Compare your answer ratings with your partner. Do you agree?

A: What do you think about Mr X's answer?
B: I have 2 stars.
A: Me too. / Really? I have …

4 Here are Jan's comments on each answer. They aren't in the correct order. Write her comments under the correct answers.

- Well that's a very good thing. Thanks!
- No problem Roger! That's OK.
- Hi! Lots of information here. Thank you.
- Me too! I love my bed.
- That's very interesting, Pete. Now I understand about the different countries.
- I know. That's a problem for me too.

● ● ○ ●

Ask Global.com

⚙ **Jan** 25 Oct 10.15am
Q: **The clocks go back one hour tonight in my country. Which other countries do this, and why?**

☺ **Roger** 25 Oct 10.25am
A: People in Europe, North America and parts of South America and Australia change their clocks. They don't change their clocks in tropical countries.

 Answer rating: ⭐⭐⭐ __ __
 ⚙ **Jan:**
 Thanks Roger. That's interesting. Do you know why?

✖ **Mr X** 25 Oct 10.27am
A: I love it! We have an extra hour in bed.

 Answer rating: __ __ __ __ __
 ⚙ **Jan:**

☺ **Roger** 25 Oct 10.42am
A: Sorry Jan, I don't know!

 Answer rating: . __ __ __ __
 ⚙ **Jan:**

♥ **Ruth** 25 Oct 10.56am
A: I hate it. I don't know how to program my DVD.

 Answer rating: __ __ __ __ __
 ⚙ **Jan:**

♠ **Pete** 25 Oct 11.19am
A: In tropical countries next to the Equator, day and night are 12 hours all year. In Britain, day and night change at different times of year. When we change our clocks we have more hours of light in the day.

 Answer rating: __ __ __ __ __
 ⚙ **Jan:**

✿ **Maxie** 25 Oct 12.10pm
A: Hi Jan!
 Where? Lots of countries.
 Why? More daytime.
 Who? Benjamin Franklin.

 Answer rating: __ __ __ __ __
 ⚙ **Jan:**

◪ **Lily from London** 25 Oct 2.46pm
A: Fantastic answers from Roger and Maxie. Another interesting thing: when we change the clocks the number of traffic accidents goes down because there's more light.

 Answer rating: __ __ __ __ __
 ⚙ **Jan:**

Global review

Vocabulary

1 Draw the times on the clocks.

three o'clock

1 a quarter to twelve
2 half past ten
3 nine forty-five
4 a quarter past seven
5 six fifteen
6 twelve o'clock

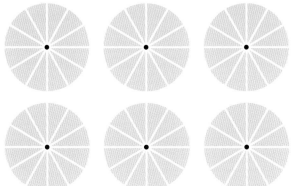

2 Match the times.

1 half past two   6.25
2 a quarter past eleven 6.35
3 ten to four   11.15
4 twenty-five past six   2.30
5 twenty-five to seven   9.45
6 a quarter to ten   3.50

3 Write the words and phrases in the box next to the correct verb.

a shower   ~~home~~   lunch   to bed
to the gym   breakfast   to work   dinner

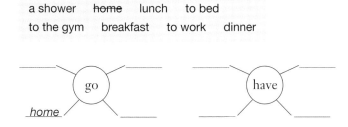

go

home

have

Grammar

1 Read the notes about a farmer's typical day. Then complete the texts with the correct verbs.

start early – have a coffee and start work – 6.00
have breakfast with Bev – 7.30
start work again – 8.15
have lunch outdoors – 1.00
go home – 6.00
have dinner with Bev – 7.00
go to bed – 10.30

Jamie is a farmer in New Zealand. He works on a sheep farm and his day _starts_ very early. He _____ a coffee and _____ work at 6 o'clock. He then _____ breakfast at about 7.30. He _____ work again at 8.15.

'I don't _____ lunch with Bev, we _____ lunch outdoors at 1 o'clock. I _____ home at 6.00. After that, I _____ dinner with Bev – at about 7.00. We _____ to bed at 10.30.'

2 <u>Underline</u> the correct words.

1 Jamie, do you like your job?   Yes, I *like / do*.
2 Does Bev have breakfast with you? Yes, she *does / have*.
3 Does she have lunch with you?   No, she *don't / doesn't*.
4 Do you go to bed after 11pm?   No, I *not go / don't*.

Listen again

1 🔘 2.34–2.37 Listen again to the speakers on page 39. Number the lines in the correct order to make sentences.

1 phone in the day and at _2_
night it isn't so expensive. _3_
I don't have time to _1_
2 because it's just ___
I like my job ___
me and my car. ___
3 to see other people. ___
we don't have time ___
I like my job, but ___
4 I think it's great. You ___
in the shop. ___
don't spend hours ___

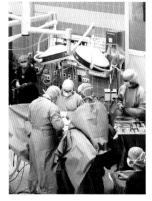

Places & People

Part 1

Vocabulary

**Places in nature
Direction words**

Listening & Reading

**UNESCO World
Heritage sites**

Reading

*Great Smoky
Mountains National
Park*

Grammar & Speaking

Question words

Writing

A place you know

Vocabulary

1 2.38 Look at the map and the pictures below. Label pictures a, e, f and g with the phrases in the box. Listen and check.

> **a river** in China   **a national park** in Spain
> **a mountain** in the US
> **an island** in Australia

2 2.39 Listen and repeat the words in **bold**.

3 Look at the map again and the compass. Are these sentences true (T) or false (F)?

1 Spain is south of the UK. ___
2 The US is east of Australia. ___
3 China is west of Kenya. ___
4 Jordan is south of Slovakia and Ukraine.
___
5 The US is north of Kenya. ___
6 The island is west of Australia. ___

Listening and Reading

1 2.40 Read and listen to *Unesco World Heritage sites* on page 43. One place on the map below is not a UNESCO World Heritage site. Which one?

2 Underline the correct answer.

1 Does UNESCO have over 840 World Heritage sites?
   Yes, it does. / No, it doesn't.
2 Does UNESCO have over 670 natural sites?
   Yes, it does. / No, it doesn't.
3 Does Italy have over 40 natural sites?
   Yes, it does. / No, it doesn't.
4 Does Australia have over 10 natural sites?
   Yes, it does. / No, it doesn't.

3 Does your country have any World Heritage or other important sites? Are they cultural or natural sites? Where are they?

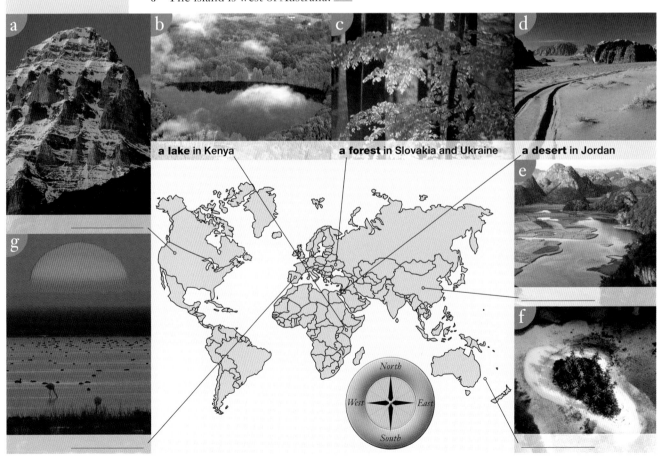

a

b

c

d

a lake in Kenya   **a forest** in Slovakia and Ukraine   **a desert** in Jordan

e

g

North

West   *East*

South

f

UNESCO World Heritage sites

A UNESCO World Heritage site is a very important cultural or natural place. There are over 670 cultural sites and over 170 natural sites. They are in 148 different countries. The country with the most cultural sites is Italy. It has 43 sites. The country with the most natural sites is Australia. It has 15 natural sites. Natural sites include forests, mountains, rivers, national parks and lakes, but not deserts.

Reading

1 Read the information in *Great Smoky Mountains National Park*. Then match the questions below to the answers.

1 When is it open?
2 Where is it?
3 What are the main attractions?
4 What's the name of the site?
5 When is a good time to visit?
6 How much is it?

2 ⬦ **2.41** Listen and check your answers. Do you think this is an interesting place to visit?

Grammar and Speaking

> ***What*** *are the main attractions?*
> ***Where*** *is it?*
> ***How much*** *is it?*
> ***When*** *is it open?*

- use question words at the start of a question

1 Complete the questions about another UNESCO World Heritage site with the words in the box.

How much	What	What	When
Where			

1 _____ is the name of the site?
   Cueva de Las Manos Pintadas.
2 _____ is it?
   Near Perito Moreno, Argentina.
3 _____ is the main attraction?
   Cave paintings from 7000 BC.
4 _____ is it open?
   From 9.00am to 7.00pm.
5 _____ is it?
   $13

2 Work in pairs. A: turn to page 97. B: turn to page 101. Talk about two more World Heritage sites from page 42.

G **Grammar focus** – explanation & more practice of question words on page 110

Writing

1 Think of a place you know. Write answers to the questions.

- What's the name of the place?
- Where is it?
- How much is it?
- When is it open?
- What are the main attractions?
- When is a good time to visit?

2 Work in groups. Read other students' descriptions. Which place would you like to visit?

> We divide the year into four seasons: *spring*, *summer*, *autumn* and *winter*. In many countries, the weather is different in each season. In the US they say *fall* not *autumn*.

Great Smoky Mountains National Park

a_____
Great Smoky Mountains National Park.

b_____
It's in the south of the US – Tennessee and North Carolina.

c_____
Nothing! The park is free.

d_____
It's open all day, every day.

e_____
The park is great for walking. There are over 500 km of walks. The mountains are very popular and the fishing is good too!

f_____
Well, it's very busy in the summer. Spring and fall are good seasons to visit. And the trees are beautiful in the fall.

Places & People

Part 2

Vocabulary
People you know

Reading
On safari

Grammar
Present simple questions

Speaking
A person you know well

colleague

boss

flatmate

neighbour

Vocabulary

1 🔊 **2.42** Look at the pictures and the diagram. Write the words *study*, *work*, or *personal life* to complete the diagram. Listen and repeat the words.

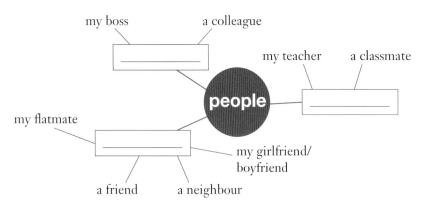

my boss   a colleague

my teacher   a classmate

people

my flatmate

my girlfriend/ boyfriend

a friend   a neighbour

2 Work in pairs. A: say a word from exercise 1. B: close your book. Listen to A and say the category. Then swap roles and repeat.

A: neighbour

B: personal life

Reading

1 Look at the picture and read *On safari* on page 45.

2 Read about Salim's life. Look at the five <u>underlined</u> sentences. Choose the one that describes each picture a, b and c.

3 Read the questions. Match the questions to Salim's answers.

Where do you work? ____
What do you do? _1_
What time do you start work? ____
Who do you live with? ____
What do you do in your free time? ____
Where are you from? ____

On safari

Wild Things organises safaris in Tanzania. Over 20 people work for the company. Salim and Cathy work for Wild Things.

Grammar

*What time **do** you start work?*
*Where **do** you work?*
*What **does** he do?*

- we use *do / does* after question words (but not with the verb *be*)
- use *do* before *I / you /we / they*
- use *does* before *he / she / it*
- use the infinitive form of the main verb

1 Put the words in the correct order to make questions.

1 does / she / What / do?
2 work / Where / she / does?
3 with / Who / does / she / work?
4 time / she / start / What / does / work?

2 Read the information about Cathy from Wild Things and answer the questions in exercise 1.

3 Write four questions using the words in the table.

What time			have breakfast?
Where			work?
When	do	you	work with?
Who			go to work?
			live with?
			go to bed?
			study English?

4 Work in pairs. Ask your partner the questions.

G **Grammar focus –** explanation & more practice of present simple questions on page 110

Salim

a

1 I'm a driver and a tour guide for Wild Things. I drive visitors to see the animals in the park.

2 I'm from Kilimanjaro in Tanzania.

3 I work in Dar es Salaam but I take the visitors to three or four different National Parks to see the animals.

4 In Dar es Salaam I start work at 8 o'clock. When I'm on safari I start work at 6 or 6.30 in the morning, it's a good time to see the animals.

5 I live alone.

6 I cook, watch TV or read books. At the weekends I go out with my friends.

b

c

Speaking

Write the name of one person you know well from Vocabulary exercise 1. Work in pairs. Ask your partner questions. Use the notes to help you.

- Who's ...?
- Where / from?
- Where / live?
- Who / live with?
- What / do?
- Where / work?
- What / do in his / her free time?

A: *Who's Keyi?*
B: *She's my neighbour.*
A: *What does she do?*
B: *She's a receptionist.*

Cathy

Cathy works in the office at the Wild Things headquarters in Dar es Salaam. She's a sales officer. She works with three colleagues, Tina, Tanya and Mariam. She answers questions about safaris from people all around the world, by email and sometimes by telephone. She works from 9.00am to 5.00pm.

1 Ask another student a question.

What's your postcode?

2 Count down from 10 to 1.

10, 9 ...

3 Say a nationality that ends with -*ian* or -*an*.

Mexican

4 Name two countries with two syllables.

Poland, ...

5 Spell a number from 11 to 20.

twenty = T-W-E-N-T-Y

18 Say this time in two different ways.

09:30

19 Ask another student about their work.

Where do you work?

20 Say three words for people you know (not family).

friend, ...

21 Say the sentence *Mary works in an office* in the negative.

6 Say three family words.

mother, ...

17 Say this time in two different ways.

01:15

It's my turn.

It's your turn.

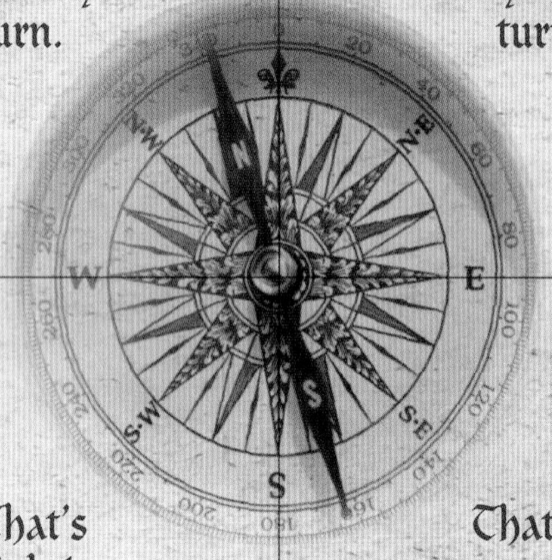

22 Ask the question *Where do you work?* in the third person (with *he / she*).

7 Say three family words beginning with *grand*.

grandmother, ...

16 Say three phrases with *go*.

go to work, ...

That's right!

That's wrong!

23 Say three question words.

what, ...

8 What is the opposite of *interesting*, *friendly* and *big*?

15 Say three phrases with *have*.

have breakfast, ...

25 Say three natural places.

river, ...

24 Say three directions.

north, ...

9 What is the opposite of *cheap*, *difficult* and *open*?

14 Say three places where people work.

hospital, ...

13 Say three sports.

football, ...

12 Say a sentence starting with *There are ...*

11 Say a sentence starting with *There isn't ...*

10 Say the numbers 13, 36, 45, 78 and 92.

Global review

Vocabulary

1 Complete the crossword puzzle with the names of the places in the pictures.

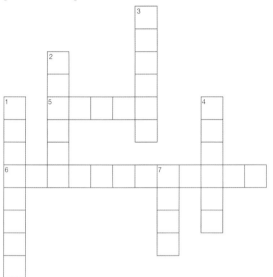

2 Complete the words from page 44.

1 She lives near me. _ e i _ _ _ o u _
2 I work with him. _ o _ _ e a _ u e
3 We listen to her in class. _ e a _ _ e _
4 I see her at the weekend. _ i _ _ _ _ i e _ _
5 We are in the same class at school. _ _ a _ _ a _ e

3 Complete the names of the seasons.

s _ _ _ _ _   s _ _ _ _ _   a _ _ _ _ _   w _ _ _ _ _

4 Complete the phrases with the verbs in the box. Then think of another example for each verb.

| go | have | like | start | study | ~~work~~ |

work in an office, with 2 colleagues, *outdoors*
1 _____ breakfast, a shower, …
2 _____ to the gym, to my English class, …
3 _____ my day, work, …
4 _____ English, Chinese, …
5 _____ Brazilian music, football, …

Grammar

Match each question word in the box to two answers.

| Who? | Where? | What time? | When? | How much? |

1 _____ My neighbour   6 _____ In summer
2 _____ $75   7 _____ 10.45pm
3 _____ Half past six   8 _____ Near London
4 _____ €2.25   9 _____ Our boss
5 _____ In a hospital   10 _____ Today

Listen again

1 ◈ 2.43 Listen to the conversation about the Great Smoky Mountains National Park from page 43. Complete the questions with question words.

A: _____'s the name of the site?
B: Great Smoky Mountains National Park.
A: _____ is it?
B: It's in the south of the US – Tennessee and North Carolina.
A: _____ is it?
B: Nothing! The park is free.
A: Wow, and _____ is it open?
B: It's open all day, every day.
A: _____ are the main attractions?
B: The park is great for walking. There are over 500 km of walks. The mountains are very popular and the fishing is good too!
A: _____ is a good time to visit?
B: Well, it's very busy in the summer. Spring and fall are good seasons to visit. And the trees are beautiful in the fall.
A: Great, thanks!

2 Listen again and check.

3 Work in pairs and practise the conversation.

In & Out

Part 1

Vocabulary & Speaking
Food

Pronunciation
Consonant clusters

Reading & Speaking
Eating in, Cuban Style

Functional language
Offering

Vocabulary and Speaking

1 Complete the labels with the words in the box.

| coffee | fish | fruit | pasta | tea |

juice

drinks

water

potatoes

meat

main course

vegetables

eggs

cheese

rice

dessert

ice cream

cakes

2 🔊 **2.44** Listen and check. Repeat the words.

3 Which food and drink from exercise 1 do you have for breakfast, lunch and dinner? Write your answers.

breakfast – juice, coffee, …

4 Work in pairs. Compare your answers. What's the same? What's different?

5 Work in pairs. Ask and answer these questions.

- Which food and drink from exercise 1 do you like?
- Which food don't you like?
- What's your favourite food and drink?

I like meat and fruit. I don't like fish. My favourite drink is coffee. And you?

Pronunciation

1 🔊 **2.45** Listen and repeat the words in the box. Be careful with the <u>underlined</u> sounds.

| br<u>ea</u>kfast | <u>eggs</u> | <u>ice</u> cr<u>ea</u>m | lun<u>ch</u> |
| ve<u>ge</u>tables | | | |

2 Work in pairs. Point to a word in exercise 1. Your partner says the word. Now it is your turn.

Eating in, **Cuban** style

A *paladar* is a Cuban restaurant. It's a restaurant but it's in a family home. The family cooks Cuban food: rice, meat, vegetables and fruit. The restaurant is a family business and the money goes to the family.

Paladar restaurants aren't big: a maximum of 12 people eat in the restaurant. Tourists and Cuban people like these restaurants because they are small and friendly and the food is very good.

You don't live in Cuba? Don't worry! There are now *paladar* home restaurants in other countries too.

Reading and Speaking

1 Look at the picture and read *Eating in, Cuban style*. What is special about paladar restaurants?

2 Read the text again. Are the sentences true (T) or false (F)?

1 A paladar is a family restaurant.
2 Paladar restaurants in Cuba make international food.
3 There are tables for 14 people.
4 Only Cuban people eat in paladar restaurants.
5 There are paladar restaurants in other countries.

3 Work in pairs. Ask and answer the questions.

- Do you think paladar restaurants are a good idea? Why / Why not?
- Are there any restaurants in family homes in your country?
- Do you invite friends and family to eat in your home? What food do you have?
- Do you like eating at home or in restaurants?

4 Work in pairs. A: turn to page 97. B: turn to page 101. Tell your partner about eating at home in another country.

Functional language

1 Read the conversation between two friends. Complete the conversation with the words in the box.

eat	have	no	Thank you	you

A: Would you like something to drink?
B: Yes, please. Do you _____ apple juice?
A: Sure. Here you are.
B: _____.
A: Would you like something to _____?
B: What's that?
A: It's Battenberg. It's a type of cake. Would _____ like to try some?
B: OK. Mmm – it's delicious.
A: Would you like some more cake?
B: Um, _____ thanks.

2 🔊 2.46 Listen and check. Do you think B likes the cake?

3 🔊 2.47 Listen and repeat the phrases from the conversation.

1 Would you like something to drink?
2 Do you have apple juice?
3 Here you are.
4 What's that?
5 It's a type of cake.

4 Work in pairs. Practise the conversation.

5 Think of different ways to complete the phrases.

Would you like …?
Do you have …?
It's a type of …
Would you like a coffee?
Would you like something to drink?

6 Work in pairs. B is at A's house. Have a similar conversation. Then swap roles and repeat.

Useful phrases

- Would you like …?
- Yes, please. / No, thanks.
- Do you have …?
- What's that?
- It's a type of …

In & Out

Part 2

Vocabulary & Pronunciation
Days of the week

Listening & Reading
Going out in London

Grammar
Adverbs of frequency

Writing
Eating out

a the cinema

b dance classes

c restaurants

d a concert

e fast food places

f the theatre

Vocabulary and Pronunciation

1 🔊 **2.48** Number the days of the week in the correct order. Then listen and check.

Wednesday ___	Monday _1_
Sunday ___	Friday ___
Thursday ___	Tuesday ___
Saturday ___	

2 Listen again and repeat. Underline the stress.

M<u>o</u>nday

3 Answer these questions with the days of the week.

- What's your favourite day?
- Which day don't you like?
- Which days do you go out with your friends and family?

4 Work in pairs. Compare your answers.

5 Which days are the weekend in your country? Work with a partner. Try to complete 1–3 below with the countries in the box.

~~Egypt~~   Jordan   Poland   Saudi Arabia

1 Thursday and Friday   _Egypt_

2 Friday and Saturday   _____

3 Saturday and Sunday   _____

Language note: we say *at the weekend* (eg Saturday and Sunday) and ***during*** *the week* (eg Monday–Friday).

Listening and Reading

1 🔊 **2.49–2.52** Look at the pictures a–f. Then listen to four people talk about going out in London. Which place do they *not* talk about?

2 Read the texts and match the speakers to the pictures.

Andrea _b_	Charlie ___
Ben ___ ___	Danny ___ ___ ___

Extend your Vocabulary – classes

I work during the day. I go to evening classes.
Complete the sentences with the words in the box.

art   computer   cookery
language   music

1 I want to learn Arabic. I go to _____ classes.

2 I like painting and drawing. I go to _____ classes.

3 I want to eat good food. I go to _____ classes.

4 I want to know more about the internet. I go to _____ classes.

5 I like singing. I go to _____ classes.

Grammar

> I **always** go to the cinema with my friends.
> On Saturday night I'm **usually** out at a concert.
> I **never** stay in at the weekend.

- use adverbs of frequency (*usually*, *always*, *never*, *sometimes* etc) before the main verb but after the verb *be*

1 Write the missing letters to complete the adverbs.

100%   _l_a_s
↓   u_ _al_y
        _o_e_ _m_s
0%   n_v_ _

2 <u>Underline</u> the best adverb to make true sentences about Andrea, Ben, Charlie and Danny.

Ben always / <u>never</u> stays in at the weekend.

1 Danny *usually / never* goes to the theatre at the weekend.
2 Charlie *usually / always* goes out to a fast food place on Fridays.
3 Andrea *sometimes / always* goes to dance classes on Wednesdays.
4 Danny *sometimes / never* has a hamburger after the theatre.

3 Add *always, usually* or *sometimes* to each of the questions below.

    usually
Do you ∧ go out at the weekend?

1 Do you go to the cinema during the week?
2 Do you go to the theatre with your family?
3 Do you go to your English classes?
4 Do you go to cafés?
5 Do you eat fast food for dinner?

4 Work in pairs. Ask your partner the questions.

A: Do you always go out at the weekend?
B: Yes, I always go out with my friends on Saturdays. We usually go to a fast food place.

G Grammar focus – explanation & more practice of adverbs of frequency on page 112

Andrea:
'On Wednesdays I go to dance classes. They're great! We do salsa. The classes are in the evening - I go with my friends after work.'

Ben:
'I never stay in at the weekend. On Saturday night I'm usually out at a concert or at the theatre.'

Charlie:
'I go out for a pizza or hamburger on Fridays. My family loves fast food!'

Danny:
'During the week I always go to the cinema with my friends. At the weekend we usually go to the theatre. We go for something cheap to eat after that –we sometimes have a hamburger.'

Time Out London £2.99 No.2043

Writing

1 Read the text about eating out and find five spelling mistakes.

Going out to eat.

I usualy go out to eat on Thusrday night. I sometimes have Italien food – I love pizza and spaghetti! My favourite restuarant is called Luigi's. I also eat a lot of Chineese food because I like rice. I never eat meat, I don't like it …

2 Choose one of the tasks below.

A Write a similar paragraph about yourself and eating out. Use adverbs of frequency.

B Write a paragraph about yourself and going out during the week. Use the texts about the four people to help you.

> '**When a man is tired of London,** he is tired of life.'
>
> Dr Samuel Johnson 1709–1784, English author and writer of *The Dictionary of the English Language.*

Global voices

Warm up

1 Look at the pictures. Complete the sentences with the words from the box.

| chicken | lamb | sushi |

1 _____ is
a type of
Japanese food.

2 _____ and _____ are types of meat.

Listening

1 🔊 **2.53–2.57** Listen to five people answer the question *What do you eat and drink at home?* Tick (✔) the food or drink they talk about.

	Katerina, Italy	Abdul, Saudi Arabia	Ryusuke, Japan	Omar, Saudi Arabia	Francesco, Italy
rice					
pasta					
coffee					
sushi					
chicken					
pizza					

2 Listen again. Are the sentences true (T) or false (F)?

1 Katerina always has breakfast at eight o'clock in the morning.
2 The main meal for Abdul is dinner.
3 Ryusuke usually has pasta or pizza for lunch.
4 Omar never has rice for lunch.
5 Francesco usually has pizza.

Language focus: *every*

Read the language note. Then put the words in the correct order.

> **Language note:** we use *every* to say when we always do something.
> *I have breakfast at 8 o'clock in the morning **every day**.*
> *I go to the cinema **every Friday**.*

every / I / pizza / day. / eat   *I eat pizza every day.*

1 eat / I / Sunday. / with my family / every
2 goes to / classes /salsa / every / She / week.
3 eat / We / Friday. / fast food / every
4 morning. / I / coffee / every / drink
5 you / day? / pasta / every / Do / eat

Speaking

Work in pairs. Ask and answer the question *What do you eat and drink at home?* Try to use adverbs of frequency and *every* in your answer.

A: What do you eat and drink at home?
B: For dinner I usually have sushi – it's a type of Japanese food. Every Sunday I eat …

Katerina, Italy | Abdul, Saudi Arabia | Ryusuke, Japan | Omar, Saudi Arabia | Francesco, Italy

Global review

Vocabulary

1 Which word is different? Give a reason.

meat, fish, pasta, cake

Cake is different because it's a dessert.
1 breakfast, dinner, café, lunch
2 juice, tea, rice, water
3 concert, theatre, cinema, office
4 pizza, pasta, spaghetti, sandwich
5 ice cream, fruit, tea, cakes

2 Correct the <u>underlined</u> words.

You go the <u>theatre</u> to watch a film.   *cinema*
1 You have <u>dinner</u> in the morning.
2 You go to a <u>cinema</u> for a coffee.
3 Banana, apple and orange are types of <u>vegetable</u>.
4 You go to <u>art</u> classes to learn French.
5 For <u>the main course</u> people eat cakes, fruit and ice cream.

3 Correct the spelling of the days of the week. Then number them in the correct order.

Munday   *Monday 1*
Wensday   —————
Saturrday   —————
Sonday   —————
Thirsday   —————
Fryday   —————
Tusday   —————

4 Work in pairs. A: say a day of the week. B: say the day before and the day after.

A: Monday

B: Sunday and Tuesday

Grammar

1 Match the words in the box with the definitions. There is one extra word.

| a sandwich | coffee | fruit | ice cream | rice |

1 People usually drink this for breakfast.
  People sometimes drink this after a meal.   —————
2 Children always like this.
  You never cook it.   —————
3 You never eat this in an expensive restaurant.
  You always make it with bread.   —————
4 You never eat this uncooked.
  People in Asia usually eat this every day.   —————

2 Put the words in the correct order.

1 at 8 o'clock. / I / always / breakfast / have
2 do / never / their English homework. / They
3 breakfast / Do / usually / you / at home? / have
4 is / sometimes / She / late for work.
5 always / This / busy / restaurant. / is / a

Listen again

1 Look at the conversation from Functional language on page 49. Number the lines in the correct order.

A: It's Battenberg. It's a special type of cake. Would you like to try some? ——
A: Would you like some more cake? ——
A: Would you like to have something to eat? ——
A: Sure. Here you are. ——
A: Would you like to have something to drink? _1_

B: Yes, please. Do you have apple juice? ——
B: Thank you very much. _4_
B: Um, no thanks. I'm fine. ——
B: What's that there? ——
B: OK. Thanks. Mmm – it's delicious. ——

2 🔊 2.58 Listen and check.

3 Listen again and cross out any extra words you **do not** hear.

Here & There

Part 1

Vocabulary
Rooms and furniture

Reading & Listening
Living underground

Grammar
Prepositions of place

Speaking
Giving opinions

Vocabulary

1 Look at the picture of the doll's house. Do you know the names of the rooms a–d? Look at the words in the box.

> bedroom   bathroom   living room
> kitchen

2 🔊 **2.59** Listen and repeat the words.

3 🔊 **2.60** Listen and repeat the rooms and furniture.

4 Are these sentences true (T) or false (F)?

In the bedroom there is a lamp and a chair. __T__

1 In the bedroom there's a TV. ___
2 In the living room there's an armchair and a lamp. ___
3 In the living room there are two sofas. ___
4 In the kitchen there's a table and chairs. ___
5 In the kitchen there's a sink. ___

5 Write some sentences about the furniture in your classroom.

In the classroom …

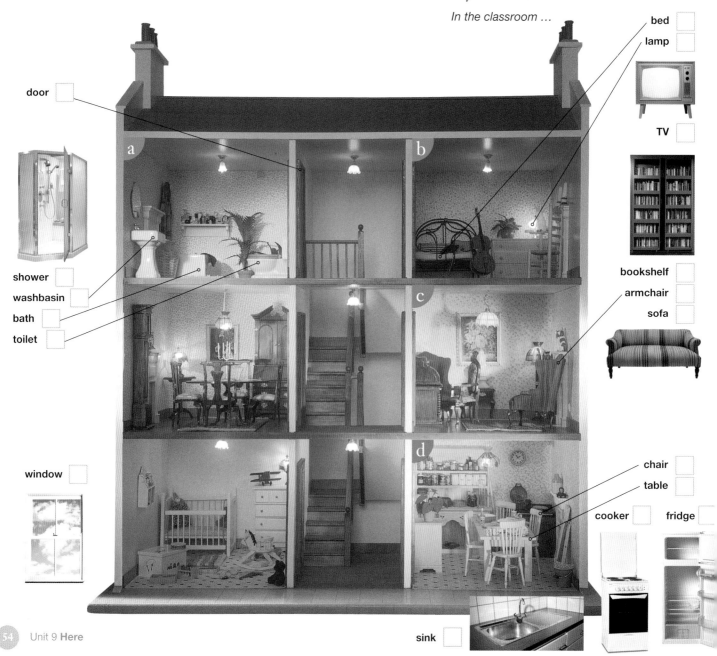

door

shower
washbasin
bath
toilet

window

bed
lamp

TV

bookshelf
armchair
sofa

chair
table
cooker   fridge

sink

Reading and Listening

1 Read the information about living underground and look at the picture of Coober Pedy. Is it a hot place or a cold place?

2 🎧 **2.61** Merv talks about his house. Listen to part 1. Why does he live in an underground house?

3 🎧 **2.62** Listen to part 2 and tick (✔) the furniture on page 54 you hear.

Grammar

> I live **in** an underground house.
> The living room is **next to** the kitchen.

- use prepositions of place (*in*, *on*, *under*, *next to*) to say where something is
- use prepositions before a noun

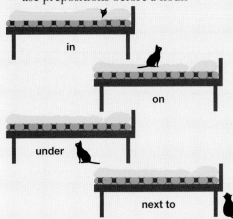

in

on

under

next to

1 Look at the pictures of Merv's house. Complete the sentences with a preposition.

The fridge is __in__ the corner.
1 The house is _____ the desert.
2 There's food _____ the table.
3 There are two books _____ the table.
4 The table is _____ the sofa.

2 🎧 **2.63** Listen to Merv talk about his bedroom. Is his bedroom picture 1 or 2?

3 Work in pairs. A: turn to page 98. B: turn to page 102. Practise describing a living room.

Ⓖ **Grammar focus** – explanation of prepositions of place on page 112

Living underground

In some countries people live in underground houses. For example, there are underground houses in Spain, Tunisia and Australia.

Merv is Australian and he lives in Coober Pedy in an underground house.

1

2

Speaking

Merv thinks living underground is fun. Work in groups. What do you think about living in these places? Tell other students in your group.

I think living …	underground	is great / boring /
	next to a river	good / terrible /
	in the mountains	bad / interesting …
	next to a park	
	in a hot / cold place	

A: *I think living underground is great. What about you?*
B: *Me, too. I think living next to a river is … / Not really. But I think living …*

Here & There

Part 2

Vocabulary & Speaking
Types of transport

Reading & Vocabulary
48 hours in Vancouver

Grammar
Imperatives

Pronunciation
Sentence stress

Functional language
Making recommendations

Writing
48 hours in...

by train | by bus | on foot
by bike | by car | by plane

Vocabulary and Speaking

1 Look at the pictures of types of transport. Which do you usually use?

2 🔊 **2.64** Listen and repeat the words.

> **Language note:** *on foot / by bike* = types of transport.
> *go for a walk / go for a bike ride* = fun, free-time activities.
> *I go to work **on foot**, but at weekends I **go for a walk** in the park.*

3 Work in pairs. Choose three questions to ask your partner.

- What type of transport is popular in your town/country?
- How do you come to the English class?
- What type of transport do you use when you go on holiday?
- Where do people go for a walk in your town?
- Do you sometimes go for a bike ride?
- What's your favourite type of transport?

Reading and Vocabulary

1 Read *48 hours in Vancouver* on page 57. Is the information for …

- business people?
- local people?
- tourists?

2 Which place or places are good if …

- you have children?
- you like shopping?
- you like art?
- you like sports?
- you want a general idea of the city?
- you want to relax?

3 Complete the phrases with words from the text.

1 Visit the lookout for _____ 360° views of the city.
2 It's a _____ place to visit.
3 This lovely park is _____ to the city centre.

4 Replace the words in **bold** with a word with the same meaning from exercise 3.

1 **near** the university
2 It's a **very interesting** part of town.
3 one of the many **wonderful** restaurants

Grammar

> *See* the city.
> *Go* shopping.
> *Don't forget* to visit Chinatown.

- use the imperative (*see, go, rent* etc) to give instructions and recommendations
- it has the same form as the infinitive
- use *don't* for the negative

1 Read the text about Vancouver again and underline all the imperative verbs.

2 Read about another part of Vancouver. Complete the text with the imperative verbs in the box.

go   go   have   visit

Visit historic **Gastown**

Gastown is the old part of Vancouver. _____ for a walk in the historic streets, _____ lunch at the Water Street Café, _____ shopping or _____ its museums and galleries. It's a fantastic place.

3 🔊 2.65 Listen and check.

ⓖ **Grammar focus** – explanation & more practice of imperatives on page 112

Pronunciation

1 🔊 2.66 Listen to these phrases and underline the stressed word in each sentence. Listen again and repeat.

go for a walk
have a coffee
take the bus
visit the park

2 Write two more imperative phrases. Work in pairs. Say your partner's phrases.

48 hours in **Vancouver**

See the city

Visit the Vancouver Lookout for fantastic 360° views of the city, mountains and the Pacific Ocean.

Visit Chinatown

Don't forget to visit Chinatown – it's a fascinating place to visit. Go shopping in the markets and eat in one of the many wonderful restaurants. When you're tired, relax in the beautiful Sun Yat Sen Chinese Garden.

See a museum

Take the bus to the Museum of Anthropology near the University. The museum has 13,000 examples of art from many cultures. The totem poles are fantastic.

Go for a bike ride

Stanley Park is a major tourist attraction. This lovely park is close to the city centre. It's a great place for all the family: there's Vancouver Aquarium and a miniature train for children, a forest with all types of animals and birds, and sports such as golf and tennis. Rent a bike – it's a very good way to see the park.

Functional language

1 Match the sentences to make recommendations. Sometimes there is more than one possibility.

1 Eat the local fish.   a It's really beautiful.
2 Go to the city museum.   b It's very cheap.
3 Look at the view.   c It's delicious.
4 Visit the national park.   d It's fantastic.
5 Go shopping in the market.   e It's very interesting.

2 Think of three recommendations of things to do in your town or country. Work in pairs. Tell your partner your recommendations.

Useful language

- Eat / Go / Look at / Visit ...
- It's beautiful / cheap / fantastic ...

Writing

1 Look again at the text about Vancouver. Write a similar text for tourists about your town or a town you know well. Remember to use imperatives and adjectives.

2 Work in pairs. Read your partner's information and think of two questions to ask. Ask your partner your questions.

Global reading

Arriving at ... **London Gatwick**

Airport Code: LGW
Distance from central London: 28 miles / 45km
Number of Terminals: 2 (North and South)
For travel information call: +44 (0)870 000 24 68.

How to get to the city centre

By _____

The Gatwick Express goes from Gatwick Airport to London Victoria train and underground station in central London.

Trains go every 15 minutes and the journey to central London takes half an hour.

First Class tickets cost £25 (single), £48 (return).

Express Class costs £17 (single), £29 (return).

Buy your ticket at the station ticket office.

By _____

There are taxis outside the airport day and night. The journey to central London takes 55–70 minutes. A London taxi takes up to 5 people.

The average cost from the airport to central London is £75–£100.

Taxi drivers take all major credit cards.

By _____

Gatwick Airport is 28 miles (45 kms) south of London. There are 4 car parks next to the airport and there are car rental offices in the North and South terminals. The journey to London takes 60–75 minutes.

All cars pay a special £8 charge to go into central London.

By _____

National Express and Easy Bus have services to central London.

Easy Bus services go every 20 minutes. The journey takes one hour and costs from £2 for internet reservations.

There is one National Express bus an hour. The journey takes 90 minutes and costs £7.60.

1 Look at the pictures and read the texts. Write the names of the forms of transport.

2 Read the texts and complete the table for the different forms of transport.

Transport				bus
Journey time		55–70 minutes		
Price			special £8 charge	
Frequency	every 15 minutes	–	–	EasyBus: National Express:

3 These 5 people all arrive in Gatwick this week. Work with a partner. Which form of transport do you recommend? Why?

1 'I'm a student. I don't have a lot of money.'

2 'My husband and our 3 small children arrive from Dubai at 2.00am. I want to get to the hotel as quickly as possible. The price isn't important.'

3 'Our hotel is in the centre of London, 5 minutes from Victoria station.'

4 'I arrive from Los Angeles at 11.30pm and the next morning I go from London to Istanbul at 7.00am. I want to go straight to the hotel. I don't have time to change money.'

5 'I arrive in Gatwick and then I plan to visit different places in the south of England – Brighton, Oxford, Bath ...'

4 Which form of transport do you prefer? Tell your partner.

I prefer ... because ...

Global review

Vocabulary

1 Does this furniture go in the kitchen (K) or the bathroom (B)?

1 a table _K_   4 a fridge ___   7 a sink ___
2 a shower ___   5 a cooker ___
3 a bath ___   6 a toilet ___

2 Read about a living room. Is it picture a, b or c?

This is the living room. There are two chairs and a sofa. There's also a small table. There's a picture, a lamp and a TV.

3 Complete the sentences with *in*, *under*, *next to* or *on*.

The cat is ___ the bed.   The cat is ___ the bed.

The cat is ___ the bed.   The cat is ___ the bed.

4 Match the words with the same meaning.

1 near   a fantastic
2 very interesting b close
3 wonderful   c fascinating

Writing

Write sentences to describe this room. Use some prepositions.

This is the …
There …

Grammar

1 Read about Hanoi. Is summer a good time to visit?

Visit the old town of **Hanoi**

The old town of Hanoi in Vietnam is very interesting. _____ shopping in the historic streets, _____ a coffee in one of the many cafés and _____ the local street food – it's wonderful! The town is small so walk or _____ a bike. When you're tired _____ under the trees in Hoàn Kiếm Lake. _____ Hanoi in the spring or autumn, it's very hot in the summer!

2 Complete the text with the verbs in the box.

| eat | go | have | relax | rent | visit |

Listen again

1 Match the beginnings and endings of these sentences from the Listening on page 55.

1 G'day! I live in   a underground house.
2 This is a town   b Coober Pedy.
3 It's in the desert and   c it's very hot in the summer!
4 I live in an   d in South Australia.
5 An underground house   e it's never very hot or very
  is great because   cold.

2 🔊 **2.67** Listen again and check your answers.

Part 1

Reading & Speaking

Ancient civilisations

Grammar

Was / were

Listening & Writing

Life in the past

Reading and Speaking

1 Work in pairs. Ask and answer the questions.

- Are there any famous historical sites in your country?
- Do you go to museums?
- Do you think history is interesting?

Useful phrases

- In my country, there are …
- I usually/sometimes/never go …
- I think history is …

2 Work in pairs. Read some facts about two ancient civilisations. A: read about the Khmer. B: read about the Maya.

3 Work in small groups. Work with students who read the same text. Decide the four most interesting facts.

I think number 3 is interesting.
Me too. / Really?

4 Work in AB pairs. Tell your partner four interesting facts about the Khmer or the Maya.

The Khmer

1 The Khmer Empire was in modern day Cambodia, and it was important from AD 802 to AD 1431.

2 Agriculture was important. The typical food was rice and fish.

3 The Khmer were great architects – there were many beautiful temples and stone carvings.

4 Angkor Wat is a famous example of a Khmer temple.

5 There were also lots of good roads.

6 The two important religions for the Khmer were Hinduism and Buddhism.

Glossary

agriculture (noun) – the work or business of farming

architect (noun) – a person who designs buildings

calendar (noun) – a system of days and dates

The Maya

1 The Mayan civilisation was in modern-day Mexico, Guatemala, Belize, Honduras and El Salvador. It was important from AD 250 to AD 900.

2 For the Mayans, vegetables were the most important food.

3 The Mayans were great architects and there are some beautiful Mayan temples today.

4 Writing was difficult because there were 800 different symbols. There were two symbols for writing numbers: and .

5 The number 5 was special for the Mayans because it's the number of fingers on a hand.

6 There was also a Mayan calendar, with 20 days in the month.

Grammar

*The number 5 **was** special.*
*They **were** great architects.*
*There **were** 20 days in the month.*

- the past of *be* is *was / were*
- use *was* with *I / he / she / it*
- use *were* with *you / we / they*
- use *there was* with singular nouns and *there were* with plural nouns

1 Read two texts about important Khmer and Mayan cities and complete the gaps with *was* or *were*.

> Angkor _____ a major city in Khmer times and is now a UNESCO world heritage site. It _____ the capital of the Khmer empire and there _____ a million people in Angkor. There _____ over 100 temples. It _____ also the location for the film *Tomb Raider*.

> Tikal _____ an important Mayan city. It _____ the political and economic capital of the region. There _____ many important temples and beautiful buildings. Some of the temples _____ in the film *Star Wars*.

2 2.68 Listen and check.

G **Grammar focus** – explanation & more practice of *was / were* on page 114

Listening and Writing

1 2.69 Look at the picture of another ancient civilisation. Can you guess where it is? Listen and check.

2 2.70 Listen to some information about this civilisation and look at the notes. Listen again and <u>underline</u> the correct words.

Notes

- *fantastic doctors / architects / teachers*
- *agriculture – important / not important*
- *typical food – bread and vegetables / bread and meat / vegetables*
- *no symbols for numbers 1–10 / 10–20 / 2–9*
- *animals – important / not important*

3 Choose **one** of the tasks below.

A Write some sentences about the ancient Egyptians. Use *was* and *were* and the notes in exercise 2 to help you.

B Write about another ancient civilisation. Use *was* and *were*.

Ancient & Modern

Part 2

Vocabulary & Listening

Adjectives
Cairo

Pronunciation

Stress & intonation

Grammar

***Was / were* negatives
and questions**

Speaking

Asking about a trip (1)

Vocabulary and Listening

1 Complete the table of positive and negative adjectives with the words in the box.

| fantastic | noisy | wonderful | terrible |

+	–
delicious	awful

2 Write another positive adjective and another negative adjective in the table.

3 Jackie was in Cairo in January. Look at the words in the box and her pictures. Which things can you see?

| the hotel | the food | the taxis |
| the people | the traffic | the River Nile |

4 2.71 Listen to Jackie talk about Cairo. Number the photos in the correct order.

5 Match the adjectives with the nouns they describe in the listening. Then listen again and check your answers.

1	hotel	a	delicious
2	museum	b	fantastic
3	food	c	modern
4	pyramids	d	wonderful
5	weather	e	cold
6	Egyptians	f	terrible
7	traffic	g	friendly
8	Nile	h	beautiful

Shopping in Cairo

There *was* / *were* many places to go shopping in Cairo. My favourite place *was* / *were* Khan al-Khalili market. It was fantastic! I *was* / *were* there in the afternoon and it was very noisy. There were many things to buy and they *wasn't* / *weren't* very expensive. There *was* / *were* lots of coffee shops, but they *were* / *weren't* very big. They were usually small and friendly.

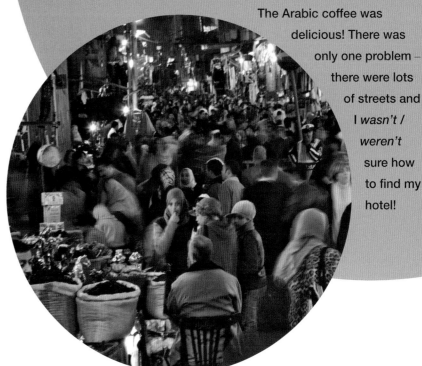

The Arabic coffee was delicious! There was only one problem – there were lots of streets and I *wasn't* / *weren't* sure how to find my hotel!

Pronunciation

1 🔊 **2.72** Listen and <u>underline</u> the stressed syllable in the adjectives.

1　That was w<u>o</u>nderful.
2　It was delicious.
3　They were fantastic.
4　They were very friendly.
5　That was terrible.
6　The taxis were awful.
7　It was really noisy too.

2 Listen again and repeat the phrases with the correct intonation.

Grammar

> It **wasn't** hot.
> There **weren't** any other tourists.
> **Was** the traffic bad? Yes, it **was**.

- use *was not* (*wasn't*) / *were not* (*weren't*) for the negative past form of *be*
- start questions with *Was* / *Were*

1 Jackie talks about shopping in *Shopping in Cairo*. <u>Underline</u> the correct words.

2 🔊 **2.73** Listen and check.

3 Jackie answers some more questions. Match the questions with the answers.

1　Were you with your family?
2　Was it an expensive trip?
3　Was the weather good?
4　Were you there in summer?
5　Were there any problems?

a　Yes, it was. It was sunny every day.
b　No, there weren't. It was a great trip!
c　No, I wasn't. I was with friends.
d　No, I wasn't. I was there in winter.
e　No, it wasn't. It was cheap.

4 🔊 **2.74** Listen and check.

Ⓖ **Grammar focus –** explanation & more practice of *was* / *were* negatives and questions on page 114

Speaking

1 Work in pairs. A: turn to page 98. B: turn to page 102. Ask your partner about another trip.

2 Write some questions to ask a partner about their last trip. Use the questions from exercise 1 to help you. Ask about …
- the weather
- the food
- the people
- the traffic

3 Work in pairs. Ask and answer your questions.

A: *Where were you?*
B: *I was in Paris.*
A: *Was the weather good?*
B: *No, it wasn't. It was terrible!*

The Global Travel Quiz

PART 1: Remember Unit 10

2.75 Listen and answer the questions. You need four correct answers to get the suitcase.

1 _____
2 _____
3 _____
4 _____
5 _____

PART 2: Odd one out

Listen to the groups of words. Write the odd one out. You need four correct answers to get the camera.

1 _____
2 _____
3 _____
4 _____
5 _____

PART 3: Where was ...?

Listen and answer the questions. You need three correct answers to get the passport.

1 _____
2 _____
3 _____
4 _____

Global review

Vocabulary and Pronunciation

1 <u>Underline</u> the correct adjective.

fantastic / <u>*noisy*</u> *traffic*
1 *delicious* / *beautiful* food
2 *great* / *easy* weather
3 *expensive* / *friendly* people
4 *busy* / *cold* markets

2 Tick (✔) the correct stress for each word.

	●·	·●·	●··
wonderful			✔
delicious			
terrible			
noisy			
fantastic			
awful			
beautiful			
friendly			

3 🔊 2.76 Listen and check.

Reading

Read the email about a trip. Was it a good trip? Choose the best answer.

a Yes, it was all fantastic.
b Yes, but there were good and bad things.
c No, it was terrible.

Hi Jackie

Dubai was really interesting. The architecture was wonderful – there were so many tall, modern buildings!

The weather wasn't good for me – very, very hot! The food was nice and there were lots of good restaurants but the traffic was very bad. The taxi drivers were terrible! It was a fantastic hotel – very big and very modern. It was near the sea and it was very beautiful at night. There were lots of shopping malls too and I was in them everyday! Everyone was really friendly.

See you soon!

Sara

Grammar and Writing

1 Put the words in the correct order to make questions.

were where you ?   Where were you?
1 good was weather the ?   _____
2 bad was traffic the ?   _____
3 hotel was expensive the ? _____
4 the nice were people ?   _____

2 Answer the questions above about a real or imaginary trip.

3 Write an email about the trip. Use *was* and *were*. Use the text in the Reading section to help you.

Listen again

1 Look at the questions and answers from page 63. Complete the sentences with *was*, *wasn't*, *were* or *weren't*.

Mike: Were you with your family?
Jackie: No, I _____. I was with friends.
Mike: Was it an expensive trip?
Jackie: No, it _____. It was cheap.
Mike: Was the weather good?
Jackie: Yes, it _____. It was sunny every day.
Mike: Were you there in summer?
Jackie: No, I _____. I was there in winter.
Mike: Were there any problems?
Jackie: No, there _____. It was a great trip!

2 🔊 2.77 Listen and check.

3 🔊 2.78 Listen and repeat the words in the box.

| was | were | wasn't | weren't |

4 Work in pairs and practise the conversation.

Part 1

Vocabulary
Years & life events

Reading & Listening
DNA: fact or fiction?
The DNA man

Grammar
Past simple

Pronunciation
Regular past simple

Writing
A biography / autobiography

Vocabulary

1 🔊 3.01 Listen and repeat the years.

1997	1973	1985	2003	2015
2010				

2 Work in pairs. Decide how to pronounce these years.

1908 ___   1998 ___
2005 ___   2012 ___
1976 _1_   1967 ___

3 🔊 3.02 Listen and number the years in exercise 2 in the order you hear them.

4 Work in pairs. Write five years. Say them to your partner. Your partner writes the years.

5 Look at the pictures and complete the expressions about life events with words from the box.

children grandchildren house married
retire school ~~university~~ work

6 Write life events in a typical order for your country. Compare your list with your partner.

Reading and Listening

1 🔊 3.03 Work in pairs. Read *DNA: fact or fiction?* on page 67. Which sentence is false? Decide with your partner then listen and check.

2 Read *The DNA man* on page 67 about Francis Crick, a scientist who discovered the structure of DNA.

3 🔊 3.04 Listen and complete Crick's biography with the missing years.

4 Number the events of Crick's life in the correct order.

He died. ___
He won the Nobel prize. ___
He studied in London and Cambridge. _1_
He had two daughters with his second wife. ___
He had his first child. ___
He started working with James Watson. ___
He worked in California. ___

Grammar

> He **finished** his PhD in 1954.
> In 1976 Crick **went** to California.

- we use the past simple (*finished*, *went*, etc) to talk about finished past actions and events
- we often say when (*In 1976 …*)
- some verbs have regular past forms (*finished*, *started*, *continued* etc) and some have irregular past forms (*went*, *got*, *met* etc)

1 Look at Crick's biography. The past simple verbs in bold are regular. What are the final two letters of the regular past simple? Write the infinitive forms.

studied   study

For more on spelling of the regular past simple, see Grammar focus on page 114.

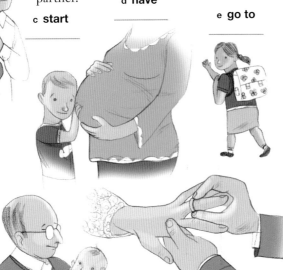

a **buy a**
_____

b **go to**
university

c **start**
_____

d **have**
_____

e **go to**
_____

f
_____

g **have** _____

h **get**
_____

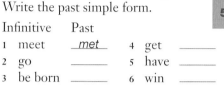

1 DNA means *deoxyribonucleic acid*.
2 DNA is in all plants and animals.
3 The police use DNA in their work.
4 The DNA of brothers and sisters is 100% the same.
5 People use DNA to test food and wine.

2 Look again at Crick's biography. The <u>underlined</u> verbs are irregular. Write the past simple form.

Infinitive	Past			
1 meet	*met*	4	get	_____
2 go	_____	5	have	_____
3 be born	_____	6	win	_____

3 Work in pairs. A: turn to page 98. B: turn to page 102. Tell your partner about another important scientist.

G **Grammar focus** – explanation & more practice of past simple on page 114

Pronunciation

1 🔊 3.05 Listen to the regular verbs in the infinitive and past simple. Notice the extra syllable /ɪd/ in *started*.

/t/	/d/	/ɪd/
finish – finished	die – died	start – started

2 🔊 3.06 Listen to the past simple verbs in the box. Tick (✔) the verbs with an extra syllable /ɪd/.

continued	ended	liked	listened
lived	repeated	visited	worked

3 Practise saying the verbs in exercise 2.

Writing

Choose **one** of the tasks below.

A Write your autobiography.

B Read the notes about another British scientist, Tim Berners-Lee. Then write his biography. Use the past simple form of the verbs.

Tim Berners-Lee

- born on 8th June 1955 / in London (be)
- his parents / computer scientists (be)
- to Oxford University (go)
- first wife Jane (meet)
- in 1980 in Geneva (start work)
- in 1989 / World Wide Web (invent)
- in 1994 / to MIT's Laboratory for Computer Science in the USA (go)
- World Wide Web Consortium (W3C) (start)

Tim Berners-Lee was born on 8th June 1955 in London.

The DNA man

Francis Crick <u>was born</u> on the 8th of June _____(1) in Northampton, England. He <u>went</u> to school in London and then **studied** physics at London University. He **continued** his research in Cambridge.

He <u>got</u> married in _____(2) and <u>had</u> a son, but he and his wife later <u>got</u> divorced. He <u>got</u> married again in _____(3) and <u>had</u> two daughters. In _____(4) he <u>met</u> another scientist, James Watson and they **started** working together. Crick **finished** his PhD in _____(5).

In _____(6), Crick, Watson and Wilkins <u>won</u> the Nobel Prize in Physiology for their research into DNA. In _____(7), Crick <u>went</u> to California to begin studies on the brain. He **died** in _____(8), aged 88.

Life & Times

Part 2

Vocabulary

Dates

Reading

Around the world in 2004

Grammar

Past simple negative

Speaking

Talking about last year

Vocabulary

1 ⟳ **3.07** Listen to the months of the year and number them in the correct order.

May ___   January _1_
December ___   April ___
June ___   November ___
February ___   July ___
October ___   March ___
August ___   September ___

2 Listen again and repeat. Notice the <u>underlined</u> stress.

3 Match the days with the dates.

1 Christmas Day   a 14 February
2 New Year's Day   b 9 May
3 Valentine's Day   c 25 December
4 Australia Day   d 1 January
5 Europe Day   e 26 January

4 ⟳ **3.08–3.12** Listen and check your answers. Is the preposition before the date *at*, *on* or *in*?

> **Language note:** we write *9th May, May 9*.
> We say *the ninth of May* or *May the ninth*.

5 ⟳ **3.13** Write the words next to the ordinal numbers. Then listen and repeat.

eighth	fifth	first	fourth	ninth
second	seventh	sixth	tenth	third

1st _____   5th _____   9th _____
2nd _____   6th _____   10th _____
3rd _____   7th _____
4th _____   8th _____

6 Write the ordinal numbers as words.

24th _twenty fourth_

1 31st _____   3 18th _____
2 22nd _____   4 23rd _____

7 Write some important dates for you. Work in pairs. Tell your partner about your dates.

A: An important date for me is 8th August.
B: Why?
A: Because it's my birthday!

Reading

1 Work with a partner. Ask and answer these questions.

- What year is it now?
- Can you remember 2004? Was it a great, good or OK year for you?
- What did you do in 2004?

In 2004 I got married / went to school …

2 Look at the pictures of events from around the world in 2004 on page 69. Do you know what the events are?

3 Read *Around the world in 2004* and match the events with the pictures a–f.

4 Read the sentences again and complete them with the phrases in the box.

age of 75	European Union
Indian Ocean	Nobel Peace
Olympic Games	White House

5 ⟳ **3.14** Listen and check.

The Berlin Wall, November 1989

Grammar

*John Kerry **didn't win** the US election.*

- use *didn't* (*did not*) before the verb to make the past simple negative
- use the infinitive form of the main verb (*like, win,* etc)

1 Are these sentences about *Around the world in 2004* true (T) or false (F)?

John Kerry won the US election. _F_

1 Wangari Maathai didn't win the Nobel Peace Prize. ___
2 Poland didn't join the European Union. ___
3 The United Arab Emirates won a medal at the Olympic Games. ___
4 Yassar Arafat died at the age of 57. ___
5 The tsunami started in the Atlantic Ocean. ___

2 Change the verbs in the false sentences to make them true.

*John Kerry **won** the US election.*
*John Kerry **didn't** win the US election.*

G **Grammar focus** – explanation & more practice of past simple negative on page 114

Speaking

1 Think about last year. What did you do? What didn't you do? Make a list.

2 Work in pairs. Tell your partner what you did and didn't do last year.

Last year was a great / good / OK year for me. In March I… On 4 April I…

> **Language note:** we use *in* to talk about months and years. We use *on* to talk about dates.
> ***In*** *March /* ***In*** *1997*
> ***On*** *4 September*

3 Can you remember what your partner said? Tell your partner. Are you correct?

A: You said last year was a good year. In January you started your English classes.
B: Yes, that's right / No, I didn't start my English classes in January, I started in February.

Around the world in 2004

1 Ten new countries, including Poland and Hungary, joined the _____ on 1 May.

2 Over 180,000 people died after an earthquake in the _____ made tsunami waves in Asia and Africa.

3 Palestinian president Yasser Arafat died at the _____.

4 The United Arab Emirates won its first medal at the _____ in Greece.

5 Wangari Maathai was the first African woman to win the _____ Prize.

6 John Kerry didn't win the US election. George W Bush won and stayed in the _____.

Global voices

Warm up

What's an important year for you? Why? Complete the sentence.

That's the year that …

Listening

1 🔊 **3.15–3.19** Listen to five people answering the question *What's an important year for you?* Match a year with a person.

1   Bea, England   2001
2   Pilar, Spain   2002
3   Carmen, Spain   1998
4   Mireille, US   2007
5   Maria, Spain   this year

2 Why is the year important for each speaker? Listen again and match the speakers 1–5 to the phrases a–e.

1   Bea, England ____
2   Pilar, Spain ____
3   Carmen, Spain ____
4   Mireille, US ____
5   Maria, Spain ____

a   She is living in London and it's very different to Spain.
b   It was the year before she started university.
c   Her son was born.
d   She went travelling around the world.
e   She moved to the United Kingdom.

Language focus

> **Language note:** we use *because* when we say why.
> 2007 was important for me **because** my son was born.

Add *because* in the correct place in each sentence.
2007 was important for me my son was born.
*2007 was important for me **because** my son was born.*

1   A memorable year was 1998 I went travelling around the world.
2   I think that is very difficult for me I am from Spain and the weather and food is very different.
3   The most important year of my life was 2001 it was the year before I started university.
4   I think probably 2002 that's the year I moved to the United Kingdom.
5   I think a memorable year would be 2007 and that's my son was born.

Speaking

Work with a partner. Ask and answer the question *What's an important year for you?* Say why.

A: What's an important year for you?
B: 2009.
A: Oh, really? Why?
B: Because that's the year I got married. What about you?

Bea, England   Pilar, Spain   Carmen, Spain   Mireille, US   Maria, Spain

Global review

Vocabulary

1 Write the missing letters to complete the words about life events.

1 st _ _ t   w _ _ k
2 h _ _ e   ch _ l d _ e _
3 _ o   _ o   u n _ v _ r _ i _ y
4 r e t _ r _
5 g _ t   m _ r r _ _ d
6 _ u y   a   h _ _ s _

2 Work in pairs. What is a good age to do the things in exercise 1?

3 One letter is missing in this series. Which one?

J F M A M J A S O N D

4 Work in pairs. A: say a month. B: say the next two months.

A: September

B: October, November

5 Write the years in numbers.

1 Nineteen oh-two _____
2 Nineteen eighteen _____
3 Nineteen seventy-two _____
4 Nineteen sixty-four _____
5 Nineteen ninety-two _____
6 Two thousand and ten _____
7 Two thousand and six _____
8 Two thousand and fourteen _____

6 Two of the years are not in the correct order. Which ones?

Grammar

1 All these verbs are in the past simple. Circle the irregular verbs.

copied	knew	met	read
remembered	repeated	spoke	
studied	went	wrote	

2 What are the infinitives of the irregular verbs in exercise 1?
For a list of irregular verbs, see page 126.

3 Work in pairs. A: say a letter and number in the table. B: say the past simple of the verb. Swap roles and repeat.

A: B-3

B: had

	A	B	C	D
1	speak	win	know	be
2	get	become	meet	come
3	see	have	give	read
4	begin	think	write	go

4 Work in pairs. A: Invent a sentence about what your partner did yesterday. Use a verb from the table. B: Listen to your partner's sentence and correct it if necessary. Then swap roles and repeat.

A: I think you read a book.

B: No, I didn't read a book, I watched TV.

B: I think you went to bed at 11 o'clock.

A: Yes, that's right!

Listen again

1 🔊 **3.20** Listen and complete the gaps with the prepositions *at*, *in*, *on* or *to*.

Francis Crick was born _____ the 8th of June 1916 _____ Northampton, England. He went to school _____ London and then studied physics _____ London University. He continued his research _____ Cambridge. He got married _____ 1940 and had a son, but he and his wife later got divorced. He got married again _____ 1949 and had 2 daughters. _____ 1951 he met another scientist, James Watson and they started working together. Crick finished his PhD _____ 1954. _____ 1962, Crick, Watson and Wilkins won the Nobel Prize in Physiology for their research into DNA. In 1976, Crick went _____ California to begin studies on the brain. He died _____ 2004, aged 88.

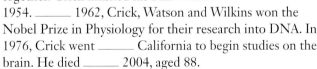

2 Look at the text again and match the prepositions with the uses.

1 at   a complete dates
2 to   b institutions
3 on   c places; years
4 in   d movement to a place

Part 1

Vocabulary
Animals

Reading & Listening
The Southern Day Frog

Grammar & Speaking
Past simple questions

Animals that disappeared

Writing
The Bali Tiger

fox

whale

bear

camel

rat

Vocabulary

1 Match an animal to its habitat.

1	A fox lives	a	in the forest.
2	A whale lives	b	near buildings.
3	A bear lives	c	in the sea.
4	A camel lives	d	in a hole underground.
5	A rat lives	e	in the desert.

2 3.21 Listen and check.

3 Work in pairs. Ask and answer the questions.

- Do you like animals?
- Which are your favourite animals?
- Which animals don't you like?

Reading and Listening

1 Read about the Southern Day Frog. Are there any Southern Day Frogs in Australia today?

2 Read the text again and complete the questions with the words in the box.

How	What	How	When	Where
~~Which~~	Why			

3 3.22 Listen and check.

4 Work in pairs. Close your book and say three things you remember about the Southern Day Frog.

The Southern Day Frog – we answer your questions

- *Which* country did it come from?
  Australia.

- _____ big was it?
  It was very small. It was 3cm long.

- _____ did it live?
  It lived in the mountains, next to small rivers.

- _____ did it eat?
  It ate insects.

- _____ did it live?
  The frog was very busy in the day. It looked for food and went into the water a lot. It also sat in the sun. At night it went under rocks to sleep.

- _____ did it disappear?
  We don't know. Some people think there was a problem with the frog's habitat.

- _____ did it disappear?
  There were a lot of frogs in the early 1970s but it disappeared in 1979.

Grammar and Speaking

1 Answer the questions about the Southern Day Frog with *Yes, it did* or *No, it didn't*. Then give the correct information for the negative answers.

Did it come from Austria?
No, it didn't. It came from Australia.

1 Did it eat plants?
   _____

2 Did it sleep at night?
   _____

3 Did it like the water?
   _____

4 Did it disappear in 1989?
   _____

2 Work in pairs. A: turn to page 98. B: turn to page 102. Find out about some more animals that disappeared.

3 🔊 3.23 Read the conversation about an animal. Find four mistakes. Then listen and check.

A: When I was little our family had a donkey.
B: Did it had a name?
A: Yes, it was Ronaldo.
B: What did it ate?
A: It ate carrots and grass.
B: When did it live?
A: It lived in the garden.
B: Did you like it?
A: Yes, I liked.

4 Think of an animal from your past. Work in pairs and ask your partner about their animal. Use the questions from the conversation to help you.

G **Grammar focus** – explanation & more practice of past simple questions on page 116

Writing

1 Complete the text about the Dodo with verbs from the box. Use the past simple.

be	come	disappear	eat	live

The Dodo _____(1) from Mauritius. It _____(2) one metre high. It _____(3) in the forest and _____(4) fruit. It _____(5) before 1700.

2 🔊 3.24 Listen and check.

3 Look at the notes about the Bali Tiger and write a paragraph about the animal. Use the paragraph in exercise 1 to help you.

The Bali Tiger …

The Bali Tiger
- Indonesia
- 1.7m long
- small island of Bali
- small animals like deer and pigs
- the 1940s

Part 2

Speaking
Visiting another country

Reading
Tribes

Listening
The TV series *Tribe*

Pronunciation
Stress and rhythm

Speaking
Asking about a trip (2)

Speaking

1 Look at the sentences about travelling. Replace the words in *italics* so they are true for you.

1 **A country I want to visit is …** *New Zealand* **because** … *I think it's very beautiful.*
2 **A country I don't want to visit is …** *Iceland* **because** … *it's very cold.*
3 **When I go on holiday I normally stay** … *in a hotel.*
4 **When I go on holiday I normally travel by** … *car.*
5 **When I visit new places, I eat** … *local food.*

2 Work in pairs. Compare your answers.

Reading

1 Read *Tribes*. Choose an interesting piece of information. Work in pairs and tell your partner the information.

Useful phrases

- I think it's interesting that …
- It's surprising/interesting/terrible that …
- I didn't know that before.

2 Read the text again and answer the questions.

1 Where is there a special TV station?
2 Which tribe has a special drink?
3 Where are there over 500 tribes?
4 Which tribe travels every year?
5 Which tribe cannot see other people for over half the year?

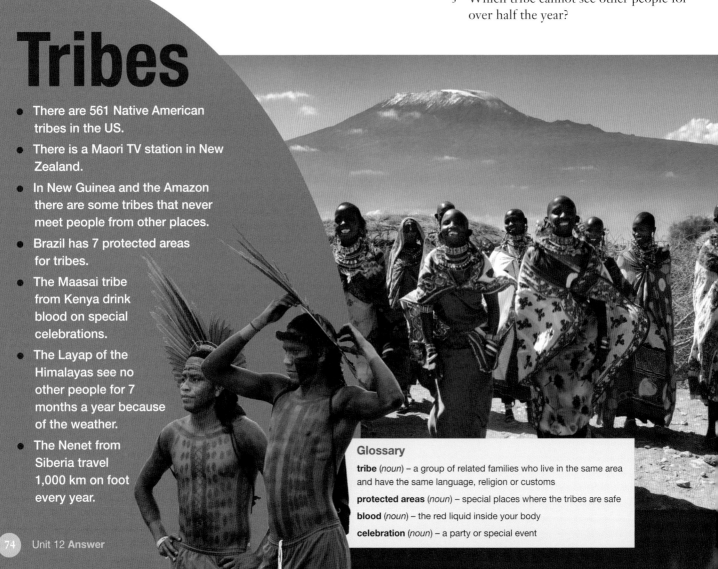

Tribes

- There are 561 Native American tribes in the US.
- There is a Maori TV station in New Zealand.
- In New Guinea and the Amazon there are some tribes that never meet people from other places.
- Brazil has 7 protected areas for tribes.
- The Maasai tribe from Kenya drink blood on special celebrations.
- The Layap of the Himalayas see no other people for 7 months a year because of the weather.
- The Nenet from Siberia travel 1,000 km on foot every year.

Glossary

tribe (*noun*) – a group of related families who live in the same area and have the same language, religion or customs

protected areas (*noun*) – special places where the tribes are safe

blood (*noun*) – the red liquid inside your body

celebration (*noun*) – a party or special event

Listening

1 Work with a partner. Look at the picture of Bruce Parry and guess the end of the sentences.

1 Bruce is …
   a an actor. b a teacher. c a TV presenter.
2 Bruce is …
   a on holiday. b at work. c at home.

2 3.25 Listen to the first part of a conversation and check your answers.

3 Match the beginning of the questions about Bruce Parry and the TV series *Tribe* to the endings.

1 What did   a he stay?
2 Where did   b have a good time?
3 Who did   c he do?
4 Where did   d he go with?
5 How long did   e he eat?
6 What food did   f he stay?
7 Did he   g he go?

4 3.26 Listen to the complete conversation. Then answer the questions.

1 lived with tribes

5 Work in pairs. Ask and answer the questions.

- Do you think the programme *Tribe* is an interesting idea?
- Are there any tribes in your country?
- Is it important to help people who live in tribes?
- Do you watch this type of programme?

Pronunciation

1 3.27 Listen and repeat the questions.

Where did you go?
How long did you stay?
What did you see?
How much did you pay?
Who did you go with?
What did you eat?
How did you get there?
Who did you meet?

2 3.28 Listen to the chant. Try and say it yourself.

Extend your Vocabulary – time

Look at the different meanings of the word *time*.
A the hours and minutes on a clock
   What time is your class?
B an occasion when you do something
   How many times did you telephone?
C to like or enjoy an experience
   Did he have a good time?

Look at the examples and decide if they have the same meaning as A, B or C above.
1 I remember the first time I went to Bali.
2 Excuse me. What's the time?
3 The last time I had pizza was in Italy.
4 We had a fantastic time at your party.

Speaking

Work in pairs. Choose **one** of the tasks below.

A A: you are a journalist. Use the questions from Pronunciation exercise 1 and your own ideas to interview B about *Tribe*.
B: you are Bruce Parry. Answer A's questions, using your imagination.

B Think about a place you visited recently, for example a town, museum, park or zoo. Ask your partner questions about their place. Use the questions in Pronunciation exercise 1 and your own ideas.

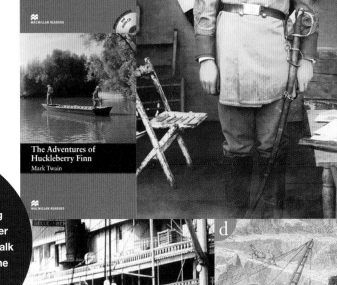

1 Look at the pictures. What do they tell you about Mark Twain's life?

2 Read about Mark Twain. Match the phrases in **bold** with the pictures. Write the correct letter next to the information.

3 Match the beginnings of the questions to the endings.

1	When was	a	have any children?
2	Where did he	b	he write his first story?
3	What did	c	live?
4	When did	d	he do?
5	Did he	e	die?
6	When did he	f	he born?

4 Read the text again and write the answers to the questions in exercise 3. The answer to one question is not in the text.

Tom Sawyer and Huckleberry Finn are two boys living near the Mississippi River in the 1840s. The books talk about their friendship, the people they meet and the adventures they have.

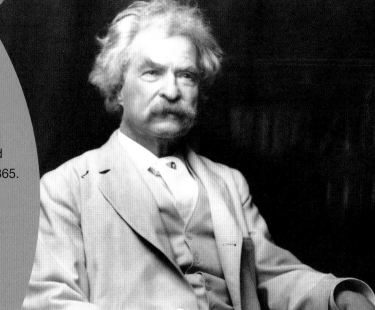

Mark Twain
1835–1910

Mark Twain was an American writer ___.
He was born on 30th November 1835, and his real name was Samuel Langhorne Clemens. He lived in Hannibal, Missouri in the United States. Hannibal is a small town on the west side of the Mississippi River.

Mark Twain had many different jobs. **He worked on the boats on the Mississippi River ___** and **he was a soldier in the US civil war ___.** He was a journalist and **he was a silver miner ___.** He wrote his first story in 1865. Two of his popular books are *The Adventures of Tom Sawyer* (1876) and *The Adventures of Huckleberry Finn* (1884) ___. He died on 21st April 1910.

Global review

Grammar

1 Find the past simple of the verbs in the box.

die   disappear   eat   get   go   join
leave   live   make   see   ~~work~~

D	I	S	A	P	P	E	A	R	E	D
I	R	J	H	S	L	O	N	D	A	A
E	W	O	R	K	E	D	A	N	T	L
D	M	I	A	Y	F	M	A	D	E	I
W	E	N	T	R	T	C	L	A	Y	V
P	I	E	C	K	Z	X	E	R	I	E
N	G	D	S	A	W	A	G	O	T	D

2 Write the questions for these answers.

1 I went to the zoo.   *Where did you go?*
2 I went with my daughter.   _____
3 We saw dolphins, bears and camels.   _____
4 We stayed there for five hours.   _____
5 We had a hamburger.   _____
6 We went on Saturday afternoon.   _____

3 Work in pairs. A: look at the phrases in list A. B: look at the phrases in list B. Ask your partner questions so they answer with the phrases in your list.

A
No, I didn't.
Yes, we did.
No, we didn't.
Yes, they did.

B
Yes, I did.
No, she didn't.
No, he didn't.
Yes, you did.

A: Did we have a class yesterday?
B: No, we didn't.

Vocabulary

1 Put the letters in the correct order to spell places where animals live.

1 eforts   2 tdsree   3 aes   4 gudrenonudr

2 Read the descriptions and write the names of the animals in the pictures.

1 This small animal is similar to a mouse. People think they're dirty.
2 This animal lives in the forest. It's sometimes dangerous.
3 This animal lives in the desert. It sometimes looks unfriendly.
4 This animal lives in the sea. It's very big.

Listen again

🔊 **3.29** In natural conversation we sometimes use extra words and phrases when we are thinking. Listen again to the conversation from page 75. <u>Underline</u> the words you **do not** hear.

A: Did you see that TV series about that man ... oh, what's his name ... Bruce Parry?
B: <u>No, I didn't.</u> Bruce Parry? Who's he?
A: He's a TV presenter. He made this incredible series called *Tribe*.
B: Oh. And what did he do?
A: Well, he lived, er, he lived with tribes ...
B: Tribes? Where? Where did he go?
A: Oh, he went to lots of different countries – Malaysia, Brazil, Russia, Tanzania ...
B: Are there tribes in all those places?
A: Yeah, it was fascinating.
B: So, who did he go with?
A: Well, obviously he went with a TV production team.
B: Yeah, OK. So, where did he stay?
A: This is the interesting thing. He stayed with a family in the tribe.
B: What, all the time?
A: Yes, day and night – and he did everything they did.

Part 1

Speaking & Vocabulary
Travelling for business

Vocabulary
Numbers over 100

Reading
Eurostar in numbers

Listening
A business trip

Grammar
Present continuous

Functional language
Buying a ticket

Speaking and Vocabulary

1 Work in pairs. Ask and answer the questions.

- Do you travel on business? Where do you go?
- Do you know someone who travels on business? Where do they go?
- Do you think business travel is interesting, exciting or boring? Why?

2 Anne Ross is a businesswoman. Look at the pictures. Underline the correct word in this sentence:

Anne is travelling around Europe by *car / train / plane*.

3 🔊 3.30 Listen and repeat the words.

Vocabulary

1 🔊 3.31 Listen and repeat the numbers.

200	500	279	564

2 Work in pairs. How do we say these numbers?

300	800	483	637	922	301

3 🔊 3.32 Listen and check.

Language note: we say *and* after *hundred*.
732 = *seven hundred **and** thirty-two*
507 = *five hundred **and** seven*

Reading

1 Read *Eurostar in numbers* on page 79. Work with a partner. Which do you think are the correct numbers in the text?

2 🔊 3.33 Listen and check.

Language note:

single ➡️　　return 🔁

Listening

1 🔊 3.34–3.36 Anne has three phone conversations with her husband, at 3.30pm, 4.25pm and 7.00pm. Listen to the conversations and number the pictures from Speaking and Vocabulary exercise 2 in the correct order.

2 🔊 3.37 Anne has a phone conversation with Mr Peeters, a business colleague. Listen and answer the questions.

1　Where is Anne now?
　　a London　b Brussels　c Moscow
2　Who is with Anne?
　　a a man　b a woman　c no-one
3　Where is she waiting?
　　a on the platform　b next to platform 6
　　c next to the ticket office

Trains

a timetable

Zeit Time Heure	Nach Destination Destination
9ʰ 10	LONDON -
9ʰ 16	LILLE E
9ʰ 25	AMIENS
9ʰ 34	ORRY CH
10ʰ 19	LONDON -
10ʰ 25	EN TETE

a platform

seats

a ticket office

Tickets

Eurostar in numbers

Eurostar is a high-speed train service. It uses the Channel Tunnel to connect London's St Pancras station with Paris and Brussels.

How fast?
London - Paris: *135 / 335* minutes
London - Brussels: *113 / 183* minutes
Top speed: *300 / 600* km per hour

How many passengers on one train?
Total number: *356 / 766*
First class: *206 / 602*
Standard class: *150 / 560*

How much?
First class single to Paris:
£260 / £360
Standard class single to Paris:
£39 / £139

Grammar

> **I'm waiting** for the train.
> The **train's arriving** now.
> **He's meeting** Anne at the station.

- we use the present continuous to say what is happening now
- form the present continuous with *be* and the main verb with *-ing*

1 Read the conversation between Anne and her husband. Where is Anne now? What is her husband doing?

Anne: Hi, John.
John: Anne! So, you made it to the hotel OK?
Anne: Yes, at last! I met Mr Peeters and everything's fine. Now I _____(1) (have) a snack in my room and I _____(2) (watch) the news on TV.
John: Oh good. So you _____(3) (rest) now.
Anne: Yes, but I _____ also _____(4) (read) a report for tomorrow's meeting.
John: You _____ always _____(5) (work), Anne!
Anne: I know, I know! How are the children?
John: They're fine, they _____(6) (play) in the garden. And I _____(7) (cook) dinner! ...

2 Read the conversation again and complete the sentences with the present continuous form of the verbs in brackets.

3 🔊 3.38 Listen and check.

Ⓖ **Grammar focus** – explanation & more practice of present continuous on page 116

Functional language

1 🔊 3.39 Read the conversation Anne had at the ticket office in London. Then listen and <u>underline</u> the correct words.

Anne: Hello, can I buy a ticket to *Bonn / <u>Brussels</u>*, please.
Ticket seller: Are you travelling today?
Anne: Yes. I think there's a train at *16.30 / 15.30*.
Ticket seller: That's right. How do you want to pay?
Anne: *Cash / Credit card*, please.
Ticket seller: That's *£206 / £307*. Thank you. Here you are.
Anne: Thanks. What time does the train arrive?
Ticket seller: *19.44 / 18.45*, and it leaves from platform *2 / 3*.
Anne: Thank you.

Language note: we use the twenty-four hour clock for timetables.
The train leaves at 06.30 (in the morning).
The train leaves at 16.30 (in the afternoon).

2 Imagine you are buying a train ticket. Replace the words in *italics* in exercise 1 with new information.

3 Work in pairs. Practise your new conversations.

Useful phrases

- Can I buy a ticket to ...
- How do you want to pay?
- In cash./By credit card.
- What time does the train leave/arrive?

Part 2

Vocabulary
Tourism

Reading & Speaking
Moscow

Listening
A bus tour of Moscow

Grammar
Present continuous negative & questions

Pronunciation
Intonation in questions

Writing
An email to a friend

Vocabulary

1 Write the words and expressions in the box next to the pictures.

| a metro station | a guidebook |
| take a bus tour | a theatre |

2 3.40 Listen and check. Do you think the vocabulary is for a business trip or a holiday?

3 Work in pairs. Cover the pictures. Can you remember ...

- four places? Which place would you like to visit?
- three things to do on holiday? Which thing do you prefer to do?
- two things to take on holiday? Which is the most important?

Reading and Speaking

1 Read the text about Moscow and write in the best phrase to complete the title.

1 a great place to do business.
2 a popular tourist destination.
3 the new destination for Chinese visitors.

2 Read the text again and answer the questions.

1 Is it true that Moscow is popular with business people and tourists?
2 How much does a typical tourist spend in Moscow?
3 Are all visitors European?

3 Work in pairs. A: turn to page 99. B: turn to page 103. Find out more about Moscow.

MOSCOW: _____

Moscow is an important city for business but it's also a popular destination for tourists. In a study it was more popular than Los Angeles or Rio de Janeiro. This is important for the Russian economy: a typical tourist spends $900 in Moscow on hotels, restaurants and entertainment. Many tourists come from Europe, but there are also lots of American and Chinese visitors.

Popular city destinations

a

a palace   take a boat trip   f   visit a gallery   g   a square

a map

Listening

1 🔊 3.41 Anne's husband John is visiting her in Moscow. He's taking a bus tour. Listen to the conversations. Tick (✔) the expressions you hear from Vocabulary on page 80.

2 Listen again and <u>underline</u> the correct words.
1 The tour costs *80 / 800* roubles.
2 The company is *Moscow Tourist Bus / Moscow City Bus Tours*.
3 The Tretyakov is an important *art gallery / science museum*.
4 John has a phone call with his *boss / wife*.
5 It *is / isn't* cold.

Grammar

> *I'm not wearing* my coat.
> She *isn't working.*
> *Are* you *eating* your lunch?
> *What* are you *doing?*
>
> • use *not* to make the present continuous negative
> • start *yes / no* questions with the verb *be*
> • you can use a short answer for *yes / no* questions (*Yes, I am / No, I'm not*)
> • use question words before the verb *be*

1 Complete the sentences with the correct form of the verb in the present continuous negative.
1 John *isn't visiting* (visit) London.
2 It isn't cold. John _____ (wear) a coat.
3 John and Anne _____ (take) the bus tour together.
4 The guide _____ (speak) Russian.

2 Make present continuous questions.
you / wear / a coat? *Are you wearing a coat?*
Where / you / sit? *Where are you sitting?*
1 you / feel / cold?
2 Who / you / work with?
3 the teacher / speak / now?

Ⓖ **Grammar focus –** explanation & more practice of present continuous negative & questions on page 116

Pronunciation

1 🔊 3.42 Listen and repeat the questions.
Are you eating your lunch? ↗
• With *yes / no* questions the intonation normally goes up.
What are you having? ↘
• With *wh-* questions the intonation normally goes down.

2 Work in pairs. Ask and answer the questions in Grammar exercise 2. Think about the intonation.

Writing

1 Read John's email to a friend about his trip to Moscow and tick (✔) the things he talks about.
1 the bus tour   5 the people
2 the hotel   6 the weather
3 the metro   7 the prices
4 the food   8 the nightlife

Hi Martin
I'm having a great time here in Moscow. Anne's in meetings all day and I'm sightseeing. Yesterday I went on a bus tour of the city, but today I'm using the metro – it's beautiful. I'm attaching a couple of photos – it's a bit different from the London Underground!
Moscow's a great place – the Kremlin's amazing. The food's good and the weather's OK. It isn't cold.
What about you? Are you having a good holiday in France?
See you Monday,
John

Glossary
attach (*verb*) – to send a document with an email

2 Imagine you are on holiday in another city. Write an email to a friend. Use the email in exercise 1 to help you.
• Describe the city.
• Say what you did yesterday.
• Say what you are doing today.

Past and present

1 **Positive** Spain in February	**2** **Negative** the sea now	**3** **Question** the theatre yesterday	**4** **Positive** the TV now	**5** **Negative** a ticket on Thursday
10 **Positive** a sandwich now	**9** **Question** school in 1985	**8** **Negative** a film now	**7** **Positive** friends at the weekend	**6** **Question** a book now
11 **Negative** Thailand in the summer	**12** **Question** an email now	**13** **Positive** a supermarket on Monday	**14** **Negative** some music now	**15** **Question** a big lunch at 1 o'clock
20 **Negative** dinner now	**19** **Positive** my job last year	**18** **Question** a computer now	**17** **Negative** a coat in winter	**16** **Positive** a car now
21 **Question** football last night	**22** **Positive** English now	**23** **Negative** $100 on 4 January	**24** **Question** the phone now	**25** **Positive** London 2009

USEFUL LANGUAGE

> My turn.   > Your turn.   > That's right!

Global review

Vocabulary

1 Work in pairs. Divide the words in the box into these three groups:

Travelling by train	Places in a city	Things you take when you travel

ticket   gallery   platform   museum   ticket office
map   palace   guidebook   seat   suitcase   theatre
timetable

2 Write the words as numbers.

four hundred and eighty-eight *488*
1 one hundred and twenty-three ___
2 two hundred and nine ___
3 six hundred and fifty ___

3 Write the numbers as words.

500   five hundred   1   376 _____   3   186 _____
2   904 _____   4   258 _____

Functional language

1 Put the conversation in the correct order.

Yes, we do. Thank you. Here are your tickets. ___
Good morning. What time's the next train to Cardiff? _1_
OK. Two tickets please. ___
Platform 5, sir. ___
That's £48 please. ___
Thank you, goodbye. Oh, which platform is it? ___
Do you take credit cards? ___
Six thirty. ___

2 ⊘ **3.43** Listen and check.

Grammar

1 Read the phone conversation. Correct the underlined phrases.

C: Emma? It's me, Christina.
E: Christina! How's Marrakesh? <u>Are you enjoy yourself</u>?
C: Yes, <u>I having</u> a great time.
E: <u>Where you are staying</u>?
C: <u>I staying</u> in a small hotel near the main square.
E: Where are you now? It's a bit noisy!
C: <u>I'm sit</u> in a café on the square. It's amazing. Lots of people are eating at street cafés, <u>some actors is telling</u> stories ... and <u>I sit</u> next to a snake charmer! What about you? <u>What are you do</u>?
E: Me? Oh, <u>I is cooking</u> dinner!

2 Choose a place from the box and imagine you are there. Write three sentences to describe what you're doing.

at the cinema   at work   in a café   in a shop
in the classroom   on a bus tour   on a plane   on a train

3 Work in pairs. Read your sentences to your partner. Your partner guesses where you are.

A: *I'm reading the menu. I'm drinking red wine. I'm eating spaghetti.*
B: *You're in an Italian restaurant.*

Listen again

1 Read the conversation between Anne and Mr Peeters from Listening exercise 2 on page 79. Complete the conversation with the words in the box.

evening   office   platform   problem
right   See   waiting   Welcome

Anne: Mr Peeters? Hello, this is Anne, Anne Ross.
Peeters: Good ___ Anne. ___ to Brussels!
Anne: Thank you, but I have a ___. I understand that someone from the ___ is meeting me at the station.
Peeters: Yes, that's ___.
Anne: Well, I'm ___ but there's no-one here.
Peeters: Don't worry, I'm coming to meet you now.
Anne: Great, I'm waiting next to ___ 6. ___ you soon.

2 ⊘ **3.44** Listen and check.

3 Work in pairs. Practise reading the conversation with your partner.

4 Cover the conversation. Try to remember the full conversation. Use the notes below to help you.

Anne: Mr Peeters? / Hello / Anne Ross.
Peeters: Good / Welcome!
Anne: Thank you / problem. Someone / office / meeting / at the station.
Peeters: Yes.
Anne: I'm waiting / no-one.
Peeters: Don't worry / I'm coming / meet.
Anne: Great / waiting / platform 6 / soon.

Part 1

Vocabulary
Colours

Reading
Wall paintings

Grammar
Describing nouns

Listening & Speaking
Two paintings

Functional language
Agreeing and disagreeing

Vocabulary

1 🔊 3.45 Look at the colour chart. Complete the sentences with the correct colours. Listen and check.

1 _____ and _____ make grey.
2 _____ and _____ make orange.
3 _____ and _____ make green.
4 _____ and _____ make purple.
5 _____ and _____ make brown.

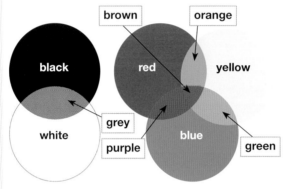

2 🔊 3.46 Listen and repeat the colours.

3 Work in pairs. Ask and answer the questions.

- What's your favourite colour?
- What colour don't you like?
- What colours do you like wearing?

Reading

1 🔊 3.47 Listen and read about different wall paintings around the world. Is this sentence true or false?

There are very old and very modern wall paintings.

2 Match the pictures of wall paintings to paragraphs 1–5 below.

3 Which colours from Vocabulary exercise 1 are not in the text?

4 Work in pairs. Ask and answer the questions.

- Do you have wall paintings in your country?
- Are they inside buildings, on street walls or on cave walls?
- Do you like them?

Paintings
on the wall

1 Diego Rivera was a Mexican painter. In the 1930s he painted the walls of the Ministry of Public Education in Mexico City. This wall painting is green, brown and yellow and has a woman working on a flower farm.

2 Many of the streets in Cuba have wall paintings. This one is blue.

3 Northern Ireland in the UK has many wall paintings. Most of the paintings are political but this wall has a popular footballer. He's wearing red.

4 The Mattancherry Palace is in Kerala, India. It's from the 16th century. Inside there are wall paintings of Hindu gods in yellow, orange and green.

5 Thousands of years ago people painted on cave walls. The paintings were usually of animals, in brown or red. These animals are from a cave in Zimbabwe, Africa.

Grammar

> *a **blue** painting*
> *There are many **wall** paintings.*
> ***interesting** wall paintings*
>
> - we can use adjectives (eg *popular, blue*) to describe nouns
> - we can also use other nouns (eg *wall*) to describe nouns
> - use adjectives and nouns **before** the main noun
> - when we use an adjective and a noun before the noun, the adjective comes first

1 Read the text about a wall painting in London. Are the <u>underlined</u> words adjectives or nouns?

In London there are many <u>wall</u> paintings in the street. My <u>favourite</u> painting is by a <u>British</u> artist called Banksy. The picture is of two <u>young</u> children. They're playing with a <u>red</u> <u>street</u> sign that says 'No <u>ball</u> games!'

2 Write the adjective or noun in the correct place.

1 I like the _blue_ wall _____ painting in Cuba. (blue)
2 He was a _____ popular _____ painter. (wall)
3 He's wearing a _____ red _____ shirt. (football)
4 Mattancherry is a/an _____ Indian _____ palace. (old)
5 I want to see the _____ cave _____ paintings. (African)
6 Cuba has lots of _____ interesting _____ art. (street)

3 🔊 3.48 Listen and check.

G **Grammar focus** – explanation & more practice of describing nouns on page 118

Listening and Speaking

1 🔊 3.49 Listen to two people talking about a painting. Which of these paintings are they talking about?

2 Match the beginnings and endings of the sentences from the conversation.

1	I like it because	a	café.
2	The painting is of	b	there's a lot of yellow in it.
3	There's a	c	chairs and tables.
4	There are some	d	a street.

3 Listen again and check.

4 Work in pairs. A: turn to page 99. B: turn to page 103. Describe a painting to your partner.

Functional language

1 Listen again to the conversation from the Listening and Speaking section. Tick (✔) the phrases you hear.

Agreeing	**Disagreeing**
I agree.	I don't agree.
Me too.	Really?
Yes, I think so.	No, I don't think so.

2 Work in pairs. Choose a picture you like from the unit. Describe the picture to your partner and say why you like it. Listen to your partner and say if you agree or disagree.

Arts & Technology

Part 2

Speaking
What we have

Vocabulary
Technology

Listening
One laptop per child

Grammar
Can/can't

Pronunciation
Can/can't

Writing
Linking words

Speaking

1 Complete the sentences so they are true for you.

- I *have / don't have* a computer in my *bedroom / living room / office*.
- I *use / don't use* a computer at *school / home / work*.
- I *like / don't like* using a computer to *work / study English / watch films*.

2 Work in pairs and compare your sentences. Are they true for your partner?

A: I have a computer in my office.

Vocabulary

🔊 **3.50** Look at the pictures of computer vocabulary. Listen and repeat the words.

a webcam

a screen

a DVD drive

a keyboard

a laptop

Name of the organisation:
One Laptop Per Child

Headquarters: Cambridge, Massachusetts (USA)

Mission: to create educational opportunities for the world's poorest children

Listening

1 Work with a partner. Look at the picture and the fact box about an organisation and answer the questions.

1 Who does the organisation help?
2 What does the organisation do?

2 🔊 **3.51** Listen to the start of a talk about the organisation and check your ideas.

3 🔊 **3.52** Look at the questions. Listen to the complete talk and underline the correct answers. Sometimes more than one answer is correct.

1 The One Laptop Per Child organisation started in …
   a 2002. b 2005. c 2008.
2 Children are using the computers in …
   a Peru. b Ethiopia. c Canada.
   d South Africa. e Afghanistan.
3 The XO computer costs about…
   a $130. b $180. c $230.
4 With the computers the children …
   a read. b use the internet.
   c take photos. d use CDs and DVDs.
5 There are problems with …
   a governments. b teachers.
   c computer companies.

Grammar

*The children **can** take photos.*
*You **can't** use CDs.*
***Can** it play DVDs? No, it can't.*

- use *can* to talk about ability
- use *can* **before** the main verb in the infinitive form without *to*
- for he / she / it use *can*, not ~~cans~~
- form the negative of can with *not / n't*
- start questions with *Can*

1 Change the sentences to make positive (+), negative (-) sentences or questions (?) with *can*.

He can speak French (?) *Can he speak French?*
1 You can speak Chinese. (-)
2 I can't drive. (+)
3 I can swim. (-)
4 Her phone can take photos. (?)
5 Can he play table tennis? (+)
6 They can play basketball. (?)

2 Look at the picture and read the text.

3 Complete the text with the positive (+), negative (-) or question (?) form of *can* and the verb in brackets.

Modern technology is great, but you _____ (1) (find -) electricity for computers and mobile phones in a desert, or at the top of a mountain. Or can you? Now you can with a pull-cord generator. Pull the cord for one minute and you _____ (2) (make +) electricity to listen to a radio for one hour or you _____ (3) (talk +) on a mobile phone for 20 minutes. But _____ (4) (use / you?) it at the top of a mountain? No problem – you can use it anywhere!

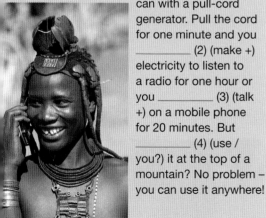

Glossary

generator (*noun*) – a machine to make electricity

Pronunciation

1 🔊 **3.53** Listen to these sentences. How do we pronounce *can* and *can't*?

You can talk on a mobile phone.
You can't find electricity in the desert.

2 Listen again and repeat the sentences.

3 🔊 **3.54** Listen to the question and short answers. How do we pronounce *can* and *can't*?

Can you speak Chinese?
Yes, I can.
No, I can't.

4 Write questions with *Can you* and the words in the box.

buy a ticket in English	drive	play table tennis
speak French	download music	

5 Work in pairs. Ask your partner your questions.

Writing

1 🔊 **3.55** Read and listen to the text about an mp3 player. Then match the linking words with the use.

I really like my mp3 player because it can do a lot of things. I use it when I'm travelling to work. I can listen to music and I can watch videos. It has a microphone and it can record short conversations but I don't usually use this. I have lots of photos on it and I can download language exercises to study on the train.

1 because   a gives more information
2 and   b gives a contrast
3 but   c says why

2 Think of a machine you have, for example a mobile phone, a laptop etc. Write a similar description. Say …

- why you like it.
- what you can or can't do with it.

Connect your ideas with *and*, *but* and *because*.

G **Grammar focus –**
explanation & more practice
of *can* on page 118

Global voices

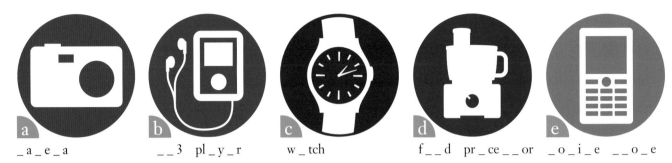

a _ a _ e _ a

b _ _ 3 pl _ y _ r

c w _ tch

d f _ _ d pr _ ce _ _ or

e _ o _ i _ e _ _ o _ e

Warm up

1 Write the missing letters to complete the names of these gadgets. Use a dictionary to help you.

2 Work in pairs. Which of the gadgets in exercise 1 do you think your partner has?

A: *I don't think you have an mp3 player.*

B: *You're wrong! / You're right!*

Listening

1 🔘 **3.56–3.59** Listen to four people answering the question *What's your favourite gadget?* Write the gadgets next to the names.

1 Nicole, Switzerland _____
2 Dorothy, Scotland _____
3 Abdul, Saudi Arabia _____
4 Marc, France _____

2 🔘 **3.60–3.63** Listen to the same people answering the question *What can you do with your mobile phone?* and tick (✔) the correct parts of the table.

	Nicole	Dorothy	Abdul	Marc
take photos / pictures	✔			
make telephone calls / call other people				
listen to music	✔			
send text messages				
send email				

Language focus

Language note: when you have one favourite, use the phrase *My favourite …* with a singular noun.
My favourite gadget *is my mobile phone because I can listen to music.*
When you have several favourites, use the phrases *One of my favourite …* with a plural noun.
One of my favourite gadgets *is my MP3 player.*

Complete the sentences with a word from the box in the singular or the plural form.

city   drink   gadget   sport

1 My favourite _____ is my laptop because I can work on the train.
2 One of my favourite _____ is swimming – I love all water sports.
3 One of my favourite _____ is Bangkok because I love Thai food.
4 My favourite _____ is coffee – I drink it all day!

Speaking

Work in pairs. Ask and answer questions.

What's your favourite gadget / sport / city / … ?

A: *What's your favourite gadget?*

B: *One of my favourite gadgets is my food processor.*

A: *Oh really, why?*

B: *Because I love cooking.*

Nicole, Switzerland   Dorothy, Scotland   Abdul, Saudi Arabia   Marc, France

Global review

Vocabulary

Look at this painting by Gauguin. Write the names of eight colours in the picture.

1 _____
2 _____
3 _____
4 _____
5 _____
6 _____
7 _____
8 _____

Speaking

Work in pairs. Describe the picture in the Vocabulary section and say why you like/don't like it. Say if you agree or disagree with your partner. Look at the phrases on page 85 to help you.

Grammar

1 Are the <u>underlined</u> words adjectives or nouns? There are three adjectives and three nouns.

1 Graham lives near a <u>flower</u> farm.
2 I'm always talking on my <u>mobile</u> phone.
3 My dad is in the <u>living</u> room watching TV.
4 Does your computer have a <u>DVD</u> drive?
5 Sarah works for a <u>computer</u> company.
6 What's your favourite <u>musical</u> instrument?

2 Put the <u>underlined</u> words in the correct order.

I really hate these <u>lessons boring science</u>.
I really hate these boring science lessons.
1 That's a <u>wall painting beautiful.</u>
2 I bought a laptop from that <u>shop computer new.</u>
3 Bilbao has a great <u>art modern museum</u>.
4 Why do you want that <u>video expensive camera</u>?
5 We have breakfast at our <u>large table kitchen</u>.

3 <u>Underline</u> the correct word.

1 My computer <u>can</u> / *can't* play CDs, **but** it *can / can't* play DVDs.
2 I like my DVD player **because** I *can / can't* record films from the TV.
3 My mobile phone is cool – I can take photos **and** I *can / can't* use the internet.
4 This is a great camera **but** you *can / can't* use it underwater.

4 Look at the words in **bold** in exercise 3. Complete the sentences about the Nano with *because*, *and* or *but*.

1 The Nano is a great car! It's very small _____ you can buy one for €1700!
2 Many people buy it _____ it's so cheap.
3 I don't usually like small cars _____ the Nano is fun to drive.
4 You can buy one in yellow _____ in many other colours too.

Listen again

1 Look at the phrases from the listening about an mp3 player on page 87. Number them in the correct order to make sentences.

1 a lot of things. _3_
   because it can do _2_
   I really like my mp3 player _1_
2 I use it when ___
   to work. ___
   I'm travelling ___
3 music and I can ___
   I can listen to ___
   watch videos. ___
4 I don't usually use this. ___
   It has a microphone and it can
   record short conversations but ___
5 to study on the train. ___
   I can download language exercises ___
   I have lots of photos on it and ___

2 🔘 **3.64** Listen and check your answers.

Language & Learning

Part 1

Vocabulary
Ways of saying numbers

Listening
Jersey

Grammar
Be going to (future)

Speaking
Disappearing languages

Writing
A Papua New Guinea language

Vocabulary

1 Match the words to the numbers.

1	twelve per cent	a	2009
2	a half	b	212
3	two thousand and nine	c	¼
4	a quarter	d	2,112
5	two hundred and twelve	e	12%
6	two thousand, one hundred and twelve	f	½

2 🔊 **3.65** Listen and repeat.

3 How do you say these sums? Are they all correct?

1 ½ + ¼ is ¾
2 50% of 90 is 45
3 84 is double 42
4 47 is half of 94

4 🔊 **3.66** Listen and check.

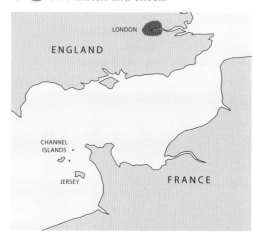

Listening

1 Look at the map and the picture of Jersey, one of the Channel Islands.

1 Which two countries is Jersey near?
2 What languages do you think they speak there?

2 Do you think these words are English?

> **Bouônjour! À bétôt.**

3 🔊 **3.67** Gemma's family comes from Jersey. Listen to Gemma talk about the languages people speak on the island. Is this sentence true or false?

Jèrriais was a local language but nobody speaks it now.

4 Listen again and answer the questions.

1 Tick (✔) the languages that people speak in Jersey.
   English   French   German
   Jèrriais   Portuguese   Polish
2 What's the population of Jersey?
3 What percentage of the population can understand Jèrriais?
4 Can Gemma speak Jèrriais now?

Extend your vocabulary – Local

Local (adjective) = connected to the place where you are or live.

Complete the sentences with the words in the box.

> radio   currency   time   calls
> language   market

1 Jèrriais is a local _____ in Jersey.
2 We arrived in New York at 3 o'clock local _____.
3 103 FM is the local _____ station.
4 I like fresh food so I shop at the local _____.
5 Using the phone is cheap because local _____ are free.
6 The local _____ is dinars but you can use dollars too.

In Papua New Guinea the national language is Tok Pisin but people speak other languages too. In Mandi, for example, some people speak Wiarumus. There are about 500 people living in Mandi and 32% speak Wiarumus. The danger level of the language disappearing is medium.

There are 841 languages spoken in Papua New Guinea.

Grammar

I think Jèrriais **is going to** *be here for some time.*
I'm going to *start classes next year.*

- use *be going to* to make predictions about the future and to talk about future plans
- use the verb *be* in the correct form (*am, is, are* etc)
- use the main verb in the infinitive form

1 3.68 Match the sentences 1–4 and a–d. Then listen and check your answers.

1 They didn't do their homework.
2 Arabic is a difficult language.
3 Jane and Tom are moving to Tokyo.
4 You didn't work very hard.

a You're going to fail the exam.
b They're going to learn Japanese.
c The teacher's going to be angry.
d I'm going to have problems learning it.

2 Complete the sentences with the correct form of *be going to*.

1 She's a great Spanish teacher. I _____ learn quickly.
2 It's quarter past five. You _____ be late for your English class.
3 It's very cold in this room. We _____ study in the library.
4 Helen has a new job in Jersey and she _____ learn Jèrriais.

G **Grammar focus** – explanation & more practice of *be going to* on page 118

Speaking

Work in pairs. A: turn to page 99. B: turn to page 103.
Read about disappearing languages.

Writing

1 Read the text above about a language from Papua New Guinea. Is the language going to disappear soon?

2 Look at the facts box below and write a paragraph about a language from the north Caucasus mountains. Look at the phrases in **red** in the Papua New Guinea text to help you.

In Russia …

There are 129 languages spoken in Russia, Georgia and Azerbaijan.

country:
Russia

national language:
Russian

region / town:
the north Caucasus mountains

name of local language:
Balkar

population:
87,000

percentage who speak the language:
97%

danger of the language disappearing:
low

Language & Learning

Part 2

Speaking & Listening

Language learning around the world

Reading

The United Kingdom of language learners

Grammar

Language review

Speaking

Giving a presentation

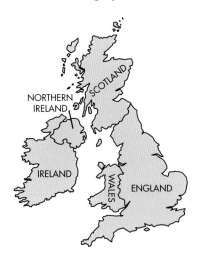

Speaking and Listening

1 Work in pairs. Guess the answers to the questions.

1 How many languages are there in the world?
   a 700   b 2500   c 7000
2 Which language has the most native speakers in the world?
   a Chinese   b English   c Spanish
3 How many people are learning Mandarin Chinese?
   a 15 million   b 30 million   c 50 million
4 What percentage of Japanese five year olds go to English conversation classes?
   a 6%   b 10%   c 21%
5 What percentage of European schoolchildren are learning English?
   a 50%   b 75%   c 90%
6 What percentage of people in Britain can count to 20 in a foreign language?
   a 5%   b 25%   c 50%

2 🔘 **3.69** Listen and check.

Reading

1 Read the introduction to *The United Kingdom of language learners* on page 93. What is the text about? Choose the correct sentence.

1 The types of English people speak in different parts of the UK.
2 The population in different parts of the UK.
3 The different languages that people speak in the UK.

2 🔘 **3.70** Read and listen to *The United Kingdom of language learners* and complete the table.

Language	How many speakers are there?	Where do they speak it?	Other information
Gaelic			
Manx			
British Sign Language		all over Britain	
Welsh			

3 Match the questions to the answers.

1 Who is learning Gaelic?
2 Who is learning Manx?
3 Who is learning BSL?
4 Who is learning Welsh?

a Deaf people.
b All schoolchildren.
c Scottish people.
d Many adults and children.

Grammar

1 Look at the text again and find two examples of these verb forms.

1 present simple *be* (British Sign Language)
   a _____   b _____
2 present simple (Gaelic)
   a _____   b _____
3 present continuous (Welsh)
   a _____   b _____
4 past simple (Manx)
   a _____   b _____

2 Complete the text below with the correct verb forms.

Punjabi:
a local language in the UK?

New languages (1) _____ (start / past simple) to arrive in Britain because of immigration. Many people (2) _____ (come / past simple) to Britain from India and Pakistan and today about 1.3 million people in the UK (3) _____ (speak / present simple) Punjabi. It (4) _____ (be / present simple) now Britain's second language. Some teachers in Britain (5) _____ (start / present continuous) to say that it is very important for children in some parts of the country to learn Punjabi.

The United Kingdom of language learners

There are about 375 million native speakers of English in the world and English is the official language in 53 countries. But what about Britain's *other* languages? The United Kingdom has a total of 16 languages. 12 are living languages that people are learning now. Two have no native speakers and two are extinct.

Welcome to Scotland
Fàilte gu Alba

Gaelic

About 60,000 people speak Gàidhlig or Scottish Gaelic, mainly in the north and west of Scotland. The word 'whisky' comes from the Gaelic word for water *uisge*. The BBC has a website for people who are learning Gaelic.

Manx

The Isle of Man is an island between England and Ireland. Officially the last Manx speaker died in 1974 and some people said the language was extinct but now many adults and children are learning Manx as a second language.

BSL

40,000 British people are first language users of British Sign Language for the deaf. BSL grammar and vocabulary is different from English. You can learn BSL online or at evening classes.

Welsh

About 750,000 people speak Welsh, the national language of Wales. The number of Welsh speakers is increasing. All school children study Welsh as a first or second language and there are Welsh radio and TV stations. Now lots of adults are learning Welsh too.

Speaking

Choose **one** of the tasks below.

A

1 Prepare a short presentation about a language you know. Try to include some of the following information.

- where people speak/spoke the language
- number of speakers
- similar to/different from other languages
- radio/TV/signs/schools
- your predictions about the future of the language

2 Give your presentation to the class.

Glossary

deaf (adjective) – a deaf person can't hear

Useful phrases

- I'm going to talk about …
- People speak/spoke … in …
- It's similar to … / It's very different from …
- There are signs/newspapers/TV programmes … in …
- I think this language is going to disappear/grow in the future.

B

1 Prepare a short presentation about language learning in your country. Try to include some of the following information.

- the languages people study now in school
- the language people studied in the past
- how adults study (in language schools, using the internet, etc)
- if people think learning languages is important

2 Give your presentation to the class.

Useful phrases

- I'm going to talk about …
- Today, children study … but in the past …
- People study …
- People in my country think …

Global reading

1 Look at the dictionary entry for *deaf*. Complete the other entries with words from the box. All the words are from this unit. Write the words in the orange boxes.

> extinct   native speaker   evening class   population
> ~~island~~   local   per cent   immigration

word   pronunciation   word class   definition
                        (noun, verb etc)

deaf /   def/   adjective   a deaf person can't hear: *Beethoven went deaf before he died.* ◄—— example

island /ˈaɪlənd/ *noun* a piece of land with sea all around: *We visited an .island.. near the west coast of Canada.*

___ /ˈləʊk(ə)l/ ___ in or related to the area where you live: *Visit your .... library.*

___ /pəˈsent/ ___ one part of every 100: *85% of people have mobile phones.*

___ /ˈiːvnɪŋ klɑːs/ ___ a class that adults go to in the evenings: *My mother is studying Spanish at an .... on Mondays.*

___ /ɪkˈstɪŋkt/ ___ if an animal or plant is ...., there are no living examples: *Many animals are now ....*

___ /ˌɪmɪˈɡreɪʃ(ə)n/ ___ the process in which people move to live in a country permanently: *The number of Spanish speakers in the USA is increasing because of ....*

___ /ˈneɪtɪv ˈspiːkə/ ___ a person who speaks a language as their first language: *There are 125 million ....s of Russian.*

___ /ˌpɒpjʊˈleɪʃ(ə)n/ ___ the number of people who live in an area: *Los Angeles has a .... of over 3 million.*

2 Write the word class of the words on the line. There are 2 adjectives; the rest are nouns.

3 Look at the three ways of recording vocabulary and find an example of …

1 using pictures.
2 writing a true example.
3 translation.

A

Dinosaurs are <u>*extinct*</u>.
I study English at an <u>*evening class*</u>.
In my country there's a lot of <u>*immigration*</u> *from Africa.*
Sicily is an <u>*island*</u>.

B

(be) extinct	*estar extinto*
evening class	*clase de adultos (de tarde)*
immigration	*inmigración*
island	*isla*

C

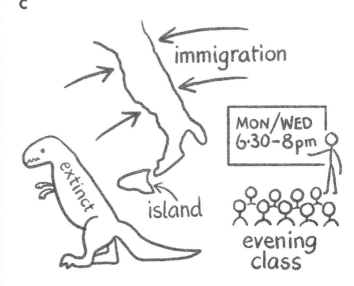

4 Work in pairs. Which example is your favourite? Why? Tell your partner.

I like … because …

5 Look at the other words in exercise 1. Prepare a vocabulary record. Use one of the examples from exercise 3 to help you, or your own idea.

Global review

Vocabulary

1 Write the words in the crossword puzzle.

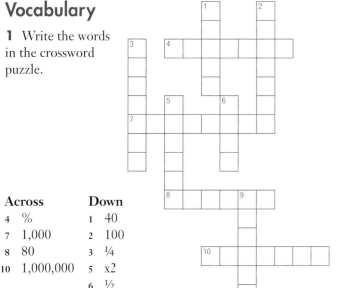

Across		Down	
4	%	1	40
7	1,000	2	100
8	80	3	¼
10	1,000,000	5	x2
		6	½
		9	12

2 Read the poem. How quickly can you say it?

One-One was a race horse
Two-Two was one too
One-One won one race
Two-Two won one too!

3 Read the number joke. Why is it funny?

Why is number 6 unhappy? Because number 7 8 9!

Grammar

Complete the sentences with the correct form of *be going to*.

1 Next year I _____ learn Japanese.
2 My brother _____ live in Australia.
3 We _____ have dinner in a restaurant tonight.
4 Some languages _____ disappear soon.
5 You _____ be late!

Listen again

1 Read the interview about Jèrriais from page 90. Then complete the interview with the correct form of the verbs in brackets.

A: Gemma, you _____ (come: present simple) from Jersey which is a small island. I know it's near France – do people speak both English and French?

B: No, English is the main language, everyone _____ (speak: present simple) English. However, there are groups of Portuguese, Polish, French and Kenyans who _____ (speak: present simple) their native languages.

A: Right.

B: There is another language called Jèrriais. It's a local language that people _____ (speak: past simple) in the past.

A: So do many people speak that today?

B: No, not really. There _____ (be: present simple) about 90,000 people in Jersey and less than 4% speak Jèrriais – and it's mainly older people. Perhaps about 15% can understand some of it.

A: Now I know many people _____ (learn: present continuous) Jèrriais. Why is that?

B: Well, for two reasons. The first is to keep the language and the culture of Jersey, and the second is for fun.

A: What about the young people – _____ (be: present simple) they interested?

B: A little, there are classes at some schools now. The government _____ (try: present continuous) to make more young people learn it.

A: A language _____ (disappear: present simple) every two weeks – is Jèrriais going to disappear?

B: I hope not. No, I think it _____ (be: going to) here for some time.

A: And what about you – do you speak Jèrriais?

B: No, I don't. But I _____ (start: going to) classes next year.

2 3.71 Listen and check your answers.

Communication activities: Student A

Unit 1, Speaking (page 7)

1 Spell the words to your partner.

1 Moscow 2 book 3 bank 4 passport 5 Mumbai

2 Listen to your partner and write the words.

1 _____ 2 _____ 3 _____ 4 _____ 5 _____

Unit 1, Reading and Listening (page 9)

1 Ask your partner *What's the postcode?* and complete the table.

Number one. What's the postcode?

Number three. What's the postcode?

1	
2	45906
3	
4	98454

5	
6	G7 9BX
7	
8	PA6 7NT

2 Answer your partner and read the postcodes.

Unit 1, Writing and Speaking (page 9)

1 Answer your partner's questions with this information.

You are Chris Hamilton
2 Station Street
Birmingham
B4 8GS
0121 344 6756

2 Ask your partner questions and complete the form on page 9.

Unit 2, Pronunciation and Speaking (page 13)

1 Write three questions to ask your partner. Use the words to help you.

from China / Italy / India …?   Are …?
a student / doctor / teacher …?   Are …?
married / single?   Are …?

2 Ask your partner your questions.

3 Read the information. Answer your partner's questions with the information.

Your name's Paula. You're a doctor from France. You're not married, you're divorced.

Unit 3, Speaking (page 18)

1 Read the description to your partner.

This is my family. This is my father. This is my sister, she's eight. This is my sister, she's twelve.

2 Listen to your partner. Tick (✔) the correct family picture.

Unit 4, Pronunciation and Speaking (page 25)

1 Complete the questions in the table with *Is there* or *Are there*.

2 Look at the information about shopping mall A. Answer your partner's questions.

B: Is there a car park?

A: Yes, there's one car park.

Questions		shopping mall A	shopping mall B
Is there	a car park?	1	
	many shops?	80	
	a cinema?	2	
	many restaurants?	15	
	many people?	yes, every day	

3 Ask your partner the questions about shopping mall B. Write the answers in the table.

Unit 5, Reading and Speaking (page 33)

1 Read the information about another race.

The Great Wall Marathon is an annual race in May. It's a full marathon of 42km running on the Great Wall of China.

2 Answer the questions in exercise 2 on page 33 about your race.

3 Tell your partner about the race.

Unit 6, Functional language (page 39)

1 Ask your partner the questions in the table. Tick (✔) the adjectives. Do you agree?

	fantastic/ great +++	good ++	OK +	bad X	terrible XX
What do you think of 24-hour shopping?					
What do you think of working at 6 o'clock in the morning?					

Useful phrases

- Yes, me too.
- Really? I think it's …

2 Listen to your partner and answer the questions.

I think it's …

Unit 7, Grammar and Speaking (page 43)

1 Look at the questions in the table. Ask your partner about their World Heritage site. Write the answers in the table. Do you think it's an interesting place to visit?

	Your site	Your partner's site
What's the name?	Fraser Island.	
Where is it?	15km east of Australia.	
How much is it?	It's free.	
When is it open?	All day, every day.	
What are the main attractions?	There are lakes, forests and beautiful beaches. You can go walking and swimming.	

2 Look at the information in the table. Answer your partner's questions about your World Heritage site.

Unit 8, Reading and Speaking (page 49)

1 Read the information about eating at home in Italy to your partner.

Eating in Italy
Italians like eating at home with family and friends. A family lunch or dinner is usually long, with lots of food. People often have pasta or rice for the main course. After that they have fruit or ice cream. Many people drink coffee after lunch or dinner.

2 Listen to your partner. Tick (✔) the correct food and drink in the table about eating in Peru.

What do people usually eat in Peru?	Main	Dessert	drinks
	fish	cheese	coffee
	chicken	fruit	tea
	pasta	ice cream	juice
	meat	cakes	
	rice		

Communication activities: Student A

Unit 9, Grammar (page 55)

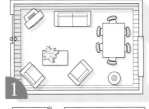

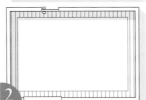

1 Look at the floor plan of a living room. Describe the room to your partner.

There's a television in the corner next to the door.

2 Listen to your partner and draw the furniture in living room 2.

Useful language

- armchairs
- a small table
- a sofa
- a plant
- a TV
- a large table
- a lamp
- chairs

Unit 10, Grammar (page 63)

1 Look at the questions in the table. Ask your partner the questions and complete the table with notes about their trip.

	Your partner's trip	Your trip
Where were you?		Bangkok, Thailand
When were you there?		In October
Was the weather good?		No – very, very hot!
Was the food good?		Yes – delicious and cheap
Were the people friendly?		Yes – very friendly
Was the traffic bad?		Yes, awful

2 Look at the notes about your trip. Answer your partner's questions with full sentences.

B: Where were you?
A: I was in Bangkok.

3 Compare your trip with your partner's. What was the same? What was different?

Unit 11, Grammar (page 67)

1 Look at the notes about Marie Curie. Tell your partner when the events happened. Use the past simple form of the verb.

Marie Curie was born in 1867 in Warsaw.

Marie Curie	year
born in Warsaw (be)	1867
physics in Paris (study)	1891
married to Pierre Curie, another scientist (get)	1895
first daughter (have)	1897
the Nobel Prize for physics (win)	1903
she (die)	1934

2 Look at the information about Jane Goodall. Listen to your partner talk about her and check they use the correct form of the verb. Complete the table with the correct years.

Jane Goodall	year
She was born in London.	
She went to Tanzania to study chimpanzees.	
She studied at Cambridge, England.	
She got married to her first husband.	
She opened the Jane Goodall Institute for chimpanzee research.	
She won a Lifetime Achievement award.	

Unit 12, Grammar (page 73)

1 Put the words in the correct order to make questions about the Pyrenean Ibex. Check your answers with another student A.

1 country from Which it come? did
 Which country did it come from?

2 big it? was How _____

3 it Where live? did _____

4 eat? What it did _____

5 did How live? it _____

6 it When disappear? did _____

2 Ask student B questions about the Pyrenean Ibex. Listen and <u>underline</u> the correct answer.

The Pyrenean Ibex

It came from Spain and *France / Portugal*.
An adult male was about *148cm / 158cm* cm long.
It lived in the *mountains / forest*.
It ate *plants / small trees*.
In the summer it lived at the *top / bottom* of the mountains and in the winter it lived at the *top / bottom*.
The last ibex died on *16 / 6* January *2000 / 2002*.

3 Now listen to student B's questions about the Baiji Dolphin. Use these notes to give full answers.

- China *It came from China.*
- about 2.5m long
- lived only in fresh water / the Yangtze River / China
- fish
- lived / groups of 3 or 4 animals
- stayed / bottom of the river / came up / eat
- 2004

4 What do you think? Why did the Pyrenean Ibex and Baiji Dolphin disappear?

Unit 13, Reading and Speaking (page 80)

1 Look at the table about Moscow and complete the questions.

Population	How many people _____?	___ million
Hotels	How many _____?	_____
Typical winter temperature	_____ the typical winter temperature?	_____°C

2 Ask your partner the questions. Listen and complete the answers.

3 Read the information below about Moscow. Answer your partner's questions.

- Moscow has five airports.
- The typical summer temperature in Moscow is about 23°C (23 degrees centigrade).
- About 4 million foreign tourists visit Moscow every year.

4 Do you want to visit Moscow? Why? Tell your partner.

Unit 14, Listening and Speaking (page 85)

1 Look at this picture and describe it to student B.

Useful phrases

- This is a painting of …
- There's a …
- There are some …
- I like it / don't like it because …

2 Now listen to student B talking about another picture. Which one are they talking about?

Unit 15, Speaking (page 91)

1 Take it in turns to read and write the words. You start. There are about *6,800 languages* in the world.
_____ 250 languages have _____ million speakers. _____ popular languages are _____ and Spanish.
_____ a language dies. _____ have less than _____. There are 357 languages _____ 50 speakers. _____ are going to _____? Is that a _____?

2 Now answer the last question with your partner.

Communication activities: Student B

Unit 1, Speaking (page 7)

1 Listen to your partner and write the words.

1 _____ 2 _____ 3 _____ 4 _____ 5 _____

2 Spell the words to your partner.

1 bus 2 Paris 3 coffee 4 hotel 5 Rome

Unit 1, Reading and Listening (page 9)

1 Answer your partner and read the postcodes.

1	22476		5	W1A 4TT
2			6	
3	37001		7	HA1 2LB
4			8	

2 Ask your partner *What's the postcode?* and complete the table.

Number two. What's the postcode?

Number four. What's the postcode?

Unit 1, Writing and Speaking (page 9)

1 Ask your partner questions and complete the form on page 9.

2 Answer your partner's questions with this information.

You are Lindsay Marsh
4 Market Street
York
YO1 7DU
01904 551 536

Unit 2, Pronunciation and Speaking (page 13)

1 Write three questions to ask your partner. Use the words to help you.

from China / Italy / India?   Are _____ ?
a student / doctor / teacher?   Are _____ ?
married / single?   Are _____ ?

2 Read the information. Answer your partner's questions with the information.

Your name's Steve. You're a student from the US. You're single.

3 Ask your partner your questions.

Unit 3, Speaking (page 18)

1 Listen to your partner. Tick (✔) the correct family picture.

2 Read the description to your partner.

This is my family. This is my mother and my father. This is my sister. She's four.

Unit 4, Pronunciation and Speaking (page 25)

1 Complete the questions in the table with *Is there* or *Are there*.

2 Ask your partner the questions about shopping mall A. Write the answers in the table.

Questions		Shopping mall A	Shopping mall B
Is there	a car park?		2
	many shops?		75
	a cinema?		4
	many restaurants?		12
	many people?		yes, at the weekend

3 Look at the information about shopping mall B. Answer your partner's questions.

A: Is there a car park?

B: Yes, there are two car parks.

Unit 5, Reading and Speaking (page 33)

1 Read the information about another race.

The Flora Women's Mini Marathon is a 10km race. It takes place in Dublin, Ireland in June. Only women run this race.

2 Answer the questions in exercise 2 on page 33 about your race.

3 Tell your partner about the race.

Unit 6, Functional language (page 39)

1 Listen to your partner and answer the questions.

I think it's …

2 Ask your partner the questions in the table. Tick (✔) the adjectives. Do you agree?

	fantastic/ great +++	good ++	OK +	bad X	terrible XX
What do you think of working at night?					
What do you think of having a 9 to 5 job?					

Useful phrases

- Yes, me too.
- Really? I think it's …

Unit 7, Grammar and Speaking (page 43)

1 Look at the information in the table. Answer your partner's questions about your World Heritage site.

	Your site	Your partner's site
What's the name?	Lake Turkana	
Where is it?	North Kenya, Africa.	
How much is it?	$15	
When is it open?	6am to 6pm.	
What are the main attractions?	You can go on safari to see lots of birds and African animals.	

2 Look at the questions in the table. Ask your partner about their World Heritage site. Write the answers in the table. Do you think it's an interesting place to visit?

Unit 8, Reading and Speaking (page 49)

1 Listen to your partner. Tick (✔) the correct food and drink in the table about eating in Italy.

	Main	Dessert	drinks
What do people usually eat in Italy?	fish chicken pasta meat rice	cheese fruit ice cream cakes	coffee tea juice

2 Read the information about eating at home in Peru to your partner.

Eating in Peru
In Peru families usually eat dinner at home with their families. They eat a lot of fish, chicken, rice and potatoes. For dessert, people eat lots of fruit and they drink lots of fruit juice – there are many different types of fruit in Peru!

Communication activities: Student B

Unit 9, Grammar (page 55)

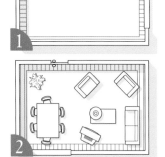

1 Listen to your partner and draw the furniture in living room 1.

2 Now describe living room 2 to your partner.

There's a plant in the corner next to the door.

Useful language

- armchairs
- a small table
- a sofa
- a plant
- a TV
- a large table
- a lamp
- chairs

Unit 10, Grammar (page 63)

1 Look at the notes about your trip. Answer your partner's questions with full sentences.

A: Where were you?

B: I was in London.

	Your trip	Your partner's trip
Where were you?	London	
When were you there?	In February	
Was the weather good?	No – cold!	
Was the food good?	Yes – good but expensive	
Were the people friendly?	Yes – very nice	
Was the traffic bad?	It was OK	

2 Ask your partner the questions and complete the table with notes about their trip.

3 Compare your trip with your partner's. What was the same? What was different?

Unit 11, Grammar (page 67)

1 Look at the information about Marie Curie. Listen to your partner talk about her and check they use the correct form of the verb. Complete the table with the correct years.

Marie Curie	year
She was born in Warsaw.	
She studied physics in Paris.	
She got married to Pierre Curie, another scientist.	
She had her first daughter.	
She won the Nobel Prize for physics.	
She died.	

2 Look at the notes about Jane Goodall. Tell your partner when the events happened. Use the past simple form of the verb.

Jane Goodall was born in London in 1934.

Jane Goodall	year
born in London (be)	1934
to Tanzania to study chimpanzees (go)	1960
at Cambridge, England (study)	1964
married to her first husband (get)	1967
the Jane Goodall Institute for chimpanzee research (open)	1977
Lifetime Achievement award (win)	2005

Unit 12, Grammar (page 73)

1 Put the words in the correct order to make questions about the Baiji dolphin. Check your answers with another student B.

1 country from Which it come? did *Which country did it come from?*
2 big it? was How _____
3 it Where live? did _____
4 eat? What it did _____
5 did How live? it _____
6 it When disappear? did _____

2 Listen to student A's questions about the Pyrenean Ibex. Use these notes to give full answers.

- Spain and France   *It came from Spain and France.*
- adult male about 148cm long
- mountains
- plants
- summer / the top of the mountains
- winter / bottom
- 6 January 2000

3 Now ask student A questions about the Baiji Dolphin. Listen and <u>underline</u> the correct answer.

The Baiji Dolphin

It came from *Japan / China*.
It was about *2.4m / 2.5m* long.
It lived in the fresh water of the *Yangtze Lake / River* in *China / Japan*.
It ate different kinds of *fish / water plants*.
It lived in small groups of *3 or 4 / 4 or 5* animals. It stayed at the bottom of the river and came up to *eat / sleep*.
The last one disappeared in *2004 / 2007*.

4 What do you think? Why did the Pyrenean Ibex and Baiji Dolphin disappear?

Unit 13, Reading and Speaking (page 80)

1 Look at the table about Moscow and complete the questions.

Airports?	How many _____?	_____
Typical summer temperature?	_____ the typical summer temperature?	_____ °C
Foreign tourists?	How _____ visit every year?	_____ million

2 Read the information below about Moscow. Answer your partner's questions.

- Moscow has a population of 9 million.
- There are 200 hotels in Moscow.
- The typical winter temperature in Moscow is about –18°C (minus 18 degrees centigrade).

3 Ask your partner the questions. Listen and complete the answers.

4 Do you want to visit Moscow? Why? Tell your partner.

Unit 14, Listening and Speaking (page 85)

1 Listen to student A talking about a picture. Which one are they talking about?

2 Now look at this picture and describe it to student A.

Useful phrases

- This is a painting of …
- There's a …
- There are some …
- I like it / don't like it because …

Unit 15, Speaking (page 91)

1 Take it in turns to read and write the words.

<u>There are about</u> 6,800 languages _____. Between 200 and _____ more than a _____. The three most _____ Chinese Mandarin, English _____.

However, every 14 days _____. 90% of languages _____ 100,000 speakers. _____ with less than _____. Which two languages _____ die this month? _____ a bad thing?

2 Now answer the last question with your partner.

Additional material

Jobs

Match the pictures with the jobs.

1 <u>den</u>tist
2 <u>doc</u>tor
3 farm <u>wor</u>ker
4 me<u>cha</u>nic
5 mu<u>si</u>cian
6 nurse
7 office <u>wor</u>ker
8 <u>sales</u> as<u>sis</u>tant
9 <u>tea</u>cher
10 <u>taxi</u> <u>dri</u>ver

Clothes

a boots	b coat	c hat	d jacket	e jumper
f shirt	g shoes	h skirt	i suit	j trousers

Phonetic symbols

Single vowels

/ɪ/	fish	/fɪʃ/	(build, England, women)
/iː/	bean	/biːn/	(he, key, niece, people)
/ʊ/	foot	/fʊt/	(could, put, woman)
/uː/	shoe	/ʃuː/	(fruit, rule, two)
/e/	egg	/eg/	(breakfast, friend, many, said)
/ə/	mother	/ˈmʌðə/	(colour, husband, police)
/ɜː/	word	/wɜːd/	(learn, skirt, birthday)
/ɔː/	talk	/tɔːk/	(four, thought, water)
/æ/	back	/bæk/	(fat, cat, bag)
/ʌ/	bus	/bʌs/	(does, onion)
/ɑː/	arm	/ɑːm/	(aunt, laugh, past)
/ɒ/	top	/tɒp/	(what, stop, hot)

Diphthongs

/ɪə/	ear	/ɪə/	(beer, here, Italian)
/eɪ/	face	/feɪs/	(eight, say, they)
/ʊə/	tourist	/ˈtʊərɪst/	(plural, sure)
/ɔɪ/	boy	/bɔɪ/	(noise, toy)
/əʊ/	nose	/nəʊz/	(know, no)
/eə/	hair	/heə/	(their, where)
/aɪ/	eye	/aɪ/	(five, buy, die, my)
/aʊ/	mouth	/maʊθ/	(town)

Consonants

/p/	pen	/pen/	(happy)
/b/	bag	/bæg/	(rabbit)
/t/	tea	/tiː/	(ate, fatter, worked)
/d/	dog	/dɒg/	(address, played)
/tʃ/	chip	/tʃɪp/	(watch, natural)
/ʤ/	jazz	/ʤæz/	(age, bridge, generous)
/k/	cake	/keɪk/	(chemistry, kitchen, cake)
/g/	girl	/gɜːl/	(foggy, dog)
/f/	film	/fɪlm/	(different, laugh, photograph)
/v/	verb	/vɜːb/	(of, very)
/θ/	thing	/θɪŋ/	(think, thin)
/ð/	these	/ðiːz/	(that, mother)
/s/	snake	/sneɪk/	(city, race)
/z/	zoo	/zuː/	(has)
/ʃ/	shop	/ʃɒp/	(description, machine, sugar)
/ʒ/	television	/teləˈvɪʒən/	(usual)
/m/	map	/mæp/	(summer)
/n/	name	/neɪm/	(sunny, knife)
/ŋ/	ring	/rɪŋ/	(sing, tongue)
/h/	house	/haʊs/	(who)
/l/	leg	/leg/	(hill, possible)
/r/	road	/rəʊd/	(carry, write)
/w/	wine	/waɪn/	(one, why)
/j/	yes	/jes/	(used)

Letters of the alphabet

/eɪ/	/iː/	/e/	/aɪ/	/əʊ/	/uː/	/ɑː/
Aa	Bb	Ff	Ii	Oo	Qq	Rr
Hh	Cc	Ll	Yy		Uu	
Jj	Dd	Mm			Ww	
Kk	Ee	Nn				
	Gg	Ss				
	Pp	Xx				
	Tt	Zz				
	Vv					

Grammar focus

Units 1 & 2

Nouns

- Form regular plural nouns like this:

most nouns	add -s	a book ——▶ books
nouns ending in -ch, -s, -sh, -x	add -es	a bus ——▶ buses
nouns ending in consonant + y	change to -ies	a country ——▶ countries

a/an

- Before nouns starting with a consonant sound use *a*.
- Before nouns starting with a vowel sound use *an*:
  an address

What's

- Use *What's ...?* to ask about things.

be (1)

- Form positive and negative sentences like this:

	Positive (+)		Negative (-)	
I	I'm	(I am)	I'm not	(I am not)
you	You're	(You are)	You aren't	(You are not)
he/she/it	He's/She's/It's Italian.	(He is/She is/It is)	He/She/It isn't Indian.	(He/She/It is not)
we	We're	(We are)	We aren't	(We are not)
they	They're	(They are)	They aren't	(They are not)

- To make questions, put the verb first:
  You are married.   *Are you married?*
- We normally use short answers:
  Yes, we are married.   *Yes, we are.*

Subject pronouns and possessive adjectives (1)

- Look at the table. After subject pronouns, use a verb; after possessive adjectives, use a noun:

Subject pronoun	Possessive adjective	
I	My	I'm from Spain. My name's Miguel.
You*	Your*	You're in class A1. Your teacher is Lucy.
We	Our	We're students. This is our class.

*use *you* and *your* for both singular and plural

Units 1 & 2 Exercises

Nouns

1 Write the plural.

book   *books*

1 passport
2 phone
3 address
4 coffee
5 bus
6 class
7 city
8 camera

What's

2 Put the questions in order to complete the conversation.

Q: name? / What's / your   *What's your name?*
A: Jill Potter.
Q: number? / your / phone / What's
A: 01202 976 422
Q: your / What's / address?
A: 19 Station Road, Poole
Q: postcode? / And / your / what's
A: BH15 7LL

be (1)

3 Match the subject and verb. Then write the contraction.

1	I	a	are	_____
2	we	b	is	_____
3	he	c	is	*She's*
4	they	d	am	_____
5	you	e	are	_____
6	she	f	is	_____
7	it	g	are	_____

4 Change the sentence according to the symbol.

He isn't a doctor.   -⟶ +   *He's a doctor.*
1 You're French.   +⟶ ?
2 Are they doctors?   ?⟶ -
3 They aren't teachers. -⟶ +
4 She isn't a student.   -⟶ +
5 I'm from Russian.   +⟶ -
6 You're in a café.   +⟶ ?

Subject pronouns and possessive adjectives (1)

5 Choose the correct word.

Teacher: Hi. *I* / My am Lucy. *I* / My am the teacher. What's *you* / your name?
Student 1: *I* / My am Andrea.
Teacher: OK. This is *you* / your book. Sit here.
Student 2: Hi Andrea. *I* / My name's Oliver and this is Susanne. *We* / Our are from Germany.
Student 3: Are *you* / your from Spain?
Student 1: No, *I* / my am from Venezuela.

6 Now write the conversation again with contractions.

Teacher: Hi. I'm Lucy …

Units 3 & 4

Subject pronouns and possessive adjectives (2)

- Look at the table:

Subject pronoun	Possessive adjective	
he	his	**He**'s my cousin. **His** name is Patrick.
she	her	**She**'s my aunt. **Her** name is Rita.
it	its	**It**'s my dog. **Its** name is Rex.
they	their	**They**'re my grandparents. **Their** names are Frank and Doris.

- Notice the pronunciation: It's = /ɪts/ = Its
  They're = /ðeə/ = Their

Possessive 's

- Use **'s** to show possession:
  It's my brother's car.

- Use **s'** for the plural:
  It's my brothers' school.

be (2)

		Negative				Question		
he	He **isn't**		(He **is not**)		**Is** he		**Yes,** he/she/it **is.**
she	She **isn't**	in London.	(She **is not**)		**Is** she	in New York?	**No,** he/she /it **isn't.**
it	It **isn't**		(It **is not**)		**Is** it		**Yes,** they **are.**
they	They **aren't**		(They **are not**)		**Are** they		**No,** they **aren't.**

There is / There are

- Form the positive with *There is* (+ singular noun) and *There are* (+ plural noun):
  There's *a cinema in the mall.*
  There are *3 restaurants.*
- To form the question, put the verb first:
  Is *there a book shop?*
  Are *there* **any** *banks?*

Units 3 & 4 Exercises

Subject pronouns and possessive adjectives (2)

1 Choose the correct form.

She / Her is my mother.

1 *He / His* is my brother.
2 *They are / Their* from Mexico.
3 *Its / It's* a photo of my family.
4 *She / Her* father's name is Jonas.

5 This is my aunt and uncle and this is *they / their* daughter.
6 My cousin is American. *She / Her* is from Hawaii.
7 Is this *he / his* wife?

Possessive 's

2 Decide if an apostrophe (') is necessary. Write it in the correct position.

I have two brothers and a sister. ✔
This is my brothers wife. ✗ *This is my brother's wife.*

1 My cousins are from Manchester.
2 She's my mothers sister.
3 My daughters names are Rhona and Maya.
4 My sisters husband is Australian.

5 My sons are students.
6 This is a photo of my fathers birthday party.
7 My brothers name is Lester.
8 My sisters husbands are teachers.

be (2)

3 Correct the sentences.

1 They are your sisters?
2 It not is my car.
3 Is she your cousin? Yes, she is my cousin.

4 They are'nt my brothers.
5 Is they your photos?
6 Is he your brother? No, isn't.

There is / There are

4 Write positive sentences.

two banks   *There are two banks.*

1 a car park
2 3 cinemas
3 a big hotel
4 a shopping mall
5 many cafés
6 8 restaurants
7 a bank
8 many bookshops

5 Write questions & answers about things in your classroom.

CD player   *Is there a CD player?   Yes, there is.*

1 DVD player
2 dictionaries
3 lots of students
4 computer
5 books
6 television
7 board
8 windows

$$12 + 3 + 5 - 7 =$$
$$78 - 5 \times 3 =$$
$$5 \times 4 \, 5 - 7 + 23 - 9 =$$

6 Complete the telephone conversation with *there is / there are / Is there? / Are there?*

A: Hi. It's me. I'm at the hotel in London.
B: Is it a big hotel?
A: Yes, _____ lots of rooms. _____ two restaurants and a café and _____ a big car park.
B: What about your room? _____ windows?
A: Yes, _____ three windows.
B: _____ a telephone?
A: Yes. And _____ a television too.

Units 5, 6 & 7

There isn't / There aren't

- Form the negative with **there isn't** (+ singular noun) and **there aren't** (any + plural noun):
  There isn't a car park at the office.
  There aren't any volunteers in the hospital.

like

- Form positive sentences with:
  I / you / we / they + **like** tennis.
  He /she /it + **likes** football.

- Form the question and short answers with auxiliary **do**:
  Do you like sport?   *Yes, I do / No, I don't.*

Present simple

- Use the present simple to describe regular, daily activities.
- In positive sentences, the verb changes after he/she/it:

Most verbs	**-s**	I/you/we/they **work**	he/she/it **works**
Verbs finishing -ch,-sh,-s, -x	**-es**	I/you/we/they **finish**	he/she/it **finishes**
Verbs finishing consonant + y	**-ies**	I/you/we/they **study**	he/she/it **studies**
Irregular verbs: do, go, have		I/you/we/they **do/go/have**	he/she/it **does/goes/has**

- Form the negative with auxiliary **do/does**.

Positive		Negative	
I/you	work	I/you	**don't** work
he/she/it	works	he/she/it	**doesn't** work
we/they	work	we/they	**don't** work

Question words

- Question words go at the start of the sentence. We write a question mark (?) at the end of the sentence.

What...? Where...? When...? Who...? How much...?	to ask about	things places time people prices

Questions with be

- With **be** the order is: Question word + verb + subject?
  What's your name?
  How much is it?

Questions with other verbs

- Use auxiliary **do/does**.
- For Yes/No questions the order is: **Do/Does** + subject + verb (+ object)?
  Do you like football?
  Does she work in an office?

- For *Wh*- questions the order is: Question word + **do/does** + subject + verb?
  Where do they live?
  When does it open?

Units 5, 6 & 7 Exercises

There isn't / There aren't

1 Choose the correct word.

There isn't / aren't a clock in the office.
1 There *isn't / aren't* any students in the school.
2 There *isn't / aren't* any retired people in our class.
3 There *isn't / aren't* a computer in the office.

4 There *isn't / aren't* any students in the basketball team.
5 There *isn't / aren't* an important race in my city.
6 There *isn't / aren't* a football in the office.

like

2 Correct the mistakes.

I ~~likes~~ football.   *I like football.*
1 My brother like cricket.
2 A: Like you running?
   B: No, I don't.
3 I likes table tennis.
4 A: Do you like swimming?
   B: Yes, I like.

5 We likes American football.
6 My mother and father likes golf.
7 A: Do you like sport?
   B: Yes, I do like.
8 My cousin like tennis very much.

Present simple

3 Correct the positive verb forms.

She ~~start~~ work at 8.00.   *starts*
1 In class we listens to the CD.
2 He haves breakfast at 7.15.
3 They likes football.
4 She watch television in the evening.
5 He gos to work at 8.30.
6 We starts class at 9.00.
7 He do sport at the weekend.
8 I works in a school.

4 Change positive to negative and negative to positive.

He likes football.   *He doesn't like football.*
I don't work in a hospital.   *I work in a hospital.*
1 I have a shower in the evening.
2 We don't live in the capital city.
3 He doesn't like basketball.
4 They go to school in the morning.
5 She doesn't have time to watch television.
6 I work in an office.
7 He doesn't study at home.
8 You have lunch in a restaurant.

5 Read the description and put the verbs in the correct forms.

My brother ___*has*___ (have) a shower at 7.00. He _____ (not/have) breakfast. He _____ (start) work at 8.30. He _____ (stop) for lunch at 12.30. He _____ (finish) work at 5.00 but he _____ (not/go) straight home; he _____ (go) to the gym. After that he _____ (go) home. In the evening he _____ (watch) television. He _____ (go) to bed at about 11.00.

Question words

6 Complete with the correct question words.

Where are you from?
1 _____'s the name of the lake?
2 _____ is a ticket for the national park?
3 _____ is the Sahara Desert?
4 _____ does the park open?
5 _____ is the park office?
6 _____ do people do in the mountains in summer?

7 Order the questions. Then answer them.

name / what's / your ?   *What's your name?   My name's (Susana)*
1 you / do / work ?
2 English / study / when / you / do ?
3 neighbour's / what's / name / your ?
4 your / like / do / boss / you ?
5 fishing / do / like / you ?
6 of / what / colleagues / are / names / your / the ?
7 park / near / do / live / you / a ?

8 Write questions for the answers

___*What's his name?*___   His name's Marco.
1 _____ He lives in Florence.
2 _____ He's a bank manager.
3 _____ He starts work at 8.00.
4 _____ He lives with his wife.
5 _____ Yes, they have a son and a daughter.
6 _____ His son's name is Giulio and his daughter's name is Paola.

Units 8 & 9

Adverbs of frequency

- We use adverbs to say how often we do something and to talk about frequency:

100%	always
75%	usually
30–50%	sometimes
0%	never

- With the verb *be*, the adverb comes after the verb: *He's **never** late for class*.
- With other verbs, the adverb comes between the subject and the verb:
  ***They never eat** pasta*.

Prepositions of place

- Use prepositions of place to say where something is.
  *The cat is **in** the bed.*
  *The cat is **on** the bed.*
  *The cat is **under** the bed.*
  *The cat is **next to** the bed.*

Imperatives

- Use the imperative to give instructions and recommendations.
- The imperative has the same form as the infinitive of the verb. It doesn't change.
  *To see – **See** the city.*
  *To go – **Go** shopping.*
  *To buy – **Buy** some bread.*
- We form the negative with ***don't***:
  ***Don't swim** after eating.*

Units 8 & 9 Exercises

Adverbs of frequency

1 Correct the sentences.

Always I have coffee for breakfast.   *I always have coffee for breakfast.*
1   We have always breakfast at home.
2   My son always is late for breakfast.
3   We have usually fruit for breakfast.
4   I have a sandwich sometimes for lunch.
5   We invite friends for dinner never.
6   We have always a pizza on Friday night.
7   It usually is a four-cheese pizza.
8   My husband cooks sometimes dinner at the weekend.

2 Re-write the sentences using adverbs so the meaning is the same.

We don't drink coffee.   *We never drink coffee.*
I have pizza about 3 or 4 times a month.   *I sometimes have pizza.*
1   We eat in a restaurant 3 times a month.
2   We don't eat Japanese food.
3   On Sundays we eat at my mother's house.
4   We have pasta 5 or 6 days a week.
5   We don't drink wine.
6   We invite friends to eat 2 or 3 times a month.

3 Add an adverb so the sentence is true for you.

I drink wine.   *I sometimes drink wine.*
1   I eat Indian food.
2   I have fruit for breakfast.
3   I drink coffee in the morning.
4   I eat at my mother's house.
5   I have a sandwich for lunch.
6   I eat at a restaurant at the weekend.
7   I cook dinner.
8   We invite friends to eat at our house.

Imperatives

4 Make some recommendations about what to do in Sydney, Australia. Match a verb to an ending.

Walk —
1   Watch
2   Swim
3   Have
4   Relax
5   Buy
6   Visit

a   a show at the Sydney Opera House.
b   the Sydney Olympic Park.
c   with a coffee at a river café.
d   some paintings.
e   across the bridge.
f   in the sea.
g   some wonderful seafood.

5 Do you think these are good or bad things to do? Make recommendations. Choose the correct imperative.

Don't take a taxi.
Take the bus. It's cheap.
1   *Buy / Don't buy* things at the hotel shop. It's expensive.
2   *Walk / Don't walk* in the park at night.
3   *Take / Don't take* photographs at the market. It's exciting.
4   *Go / Don't go* in December. It's sunny.
5   *Swim / Don't swim* in the river. It's very cold.
6   *Ask / Don't ask* the police for help. They're friendly.
7   *Go / Don't go* to the shopping malls. There are many interesting shops.
8   *Have / Don't* have dinner at the hotel. The restaurant's terrible.

6 Match an instruction to a picture.

Don't drive fast.   Don't go.   ~~Don't run.~~   Don't smoke.
Don't swim.   Don't talk.   Don't walk.

Don't run.

Past simple (1) *was/were*

- Form positive sentences in the past like this:

	Positive
I	I **was**
you	You **were**
he/she/it	He/She/It **was**
we	We **were**
you	You **were**
they	They **were**

- ***There was*** + singular:
  There was a teacher *in the classroom.*
- ***There were*** + plural:
  There were 10 students *in the classroom.*

- Form the negative with ***not***:

	Negative
I	I **wasn't**
you	You **weren't**
he/she/it	He/She/It **wasn't**
we	We **weren't**
you	You **weren't**
they	They **weren't**

- To make questions, put the verb first:
  You were on holiday. ⟶ ***Were you*** *on holiday?*
- We normally use short answers:
  No, I wasn't on holiday. ⟶ ***No****, I wasn't.*

Past simple (2)

- Use the past simple to talk about finished past actions and events.
- We usually say when something happened: *I started university **last year**. I didn't meet my friends **at the weekend**.*
- In positive sentences the verb doesn't change. Form the negative with the auxiliary ***didn't***:

Positive		Negative	
I you he/she/it we they	**started** **met**	I you he/she/it we they	**didn't start** **didn't meet**

Regular verbs

To form the past simple of regular verbs:
- Most verbs, add ***-ed***: start - start***ed***; finish – finish***ed***
- Verbs ending in -*e*, add ***-d***: die – die***d***
- Verbs ending in -*y*, change -*y* to ***-ied***: study – stud***ied***

Irregular verbs

Many common verbs are irregular.

Infinitive	Past simple
be born	was born
come	came
get	got
go	went
have	had
know	knew
make	made
meet	met
read /ri:d/	read /red/
speak	spoke
win	won
write	wrote

For a complete list of irregular verbs, see page 126.

Units 10 & 11 Exercises

Past simple (1) *was/were*

1 Choose the correct form.

I was / were in the temple yesterday.
1   My grandfather *was / were* a doctor.
2   Vegetables *was / were* very important for the Mayans.
3   The typical food for the Khmer *was / were* rice.
4   There *was / were* fantastic architects in Egypt.
5   We *was / were* at the Pyramids last week.
6   There *was / were* good weather.
7   My sister *was / were* on a horse.
8   I *was / were* on a camel.

2 Complete the questions with *was* or *were*.

On your holiday, __was__ the food good?
1   _____ the people friendly?
2   _____ the traffic bad?
3   _____ the restaurants cheap?
4   _____ your sister with you?
5   _____ you in a good hotel?
6   _____ you happy to come home?

3 Complete the answers to the questions in exercise 2 with *was / were / wasn't* or *weren't*

Yes, it __was__
1   Yes, they _____
2   No, it _____
3   No, they _____
4   Yes, she _____
5   Yes, we _____
6   No, I _____

Past simple (2)

4 Put the verbs in the correct forms.

On Monday I __did__ (do) my homework.
1   In March I _____ (start) university.
2   I _____ (study) French and German.
3   There were many students and we _____ (work) very hard.
4   I _____ (meet) some interesting people.
5   One student was from Australia. She _____ (like) me very much.
6   I _____ (begin) to see her every day.
7   We _____ (go) to restaurants and the cinema together.
8   We _____ (get married) in November.

5 Decide if the underlined verbs are right or wrong. Correct the wrong verbs.

He studyed languages at university.   ✗   *studied*
1   She moved to Canada in 2009.
2   They invented a good way to do less work.
3   My grandparents deid in 1998.
4   Well done! You winned the election!
5   My father stoped work last month.
6   We becomed the first students to study in space.
7   It's good that you decided to leave your job.
8   I continued my job but I'm unhappy.

6 Change positive to negative and negative to positive.

She liked the teacher.   *She didn't like the teacher.*
We didn't come first.   *We came first.*
1   My parents got married in 1965.
2   I didn't pass my exam.
3   He wanted to be a politician.
4   They went to a football match.
5   We didn't have a good time.
6   My grandmother spoke French.

Past simple (3) questions

- Form the question with question word + **did** + subject + infinitive:

What		I	
When		you	
Where	**did**	he/she/it	eat?
How		we	
Which (food)		you	
Why		they	

- For Yes / No questions don't use the question word:

	I	
	you	
Did	he/she/it	eat?
	we	
	you	
	they	

Present continuous

- We use the present continuous to talk about things now.
- Form the present continuous with **be** and verb + **-ing**

	Positive
I	**I'm reading**
you	**You're writing**
he/she/it	**He's/She's/It's eating**
we	**We're watching** TV
you	**You're having** breakfast
they	**They're playing** football

- Form the negative with **not**:

	Negative
I	**I'm not reading**
you	**You're not writing**
he/she/it	**He's/She's/It's not eating**
we	**We're not watching** TV
you	**You're not having** breakfast
they	**They're not playing** football

- To make questions, put the verb **be** first:
  She's listening to the radio ⟶ **Is** *she listening to the radio?*
- We normally use short answers:
  Yes, she's listening to the radio. ⟶ **Yes**, *she* **is**.

Units 12 & 13 Exercises

Past simple (3) Questions

1 Match the question to an answer.

Where did you go at the weekend?
1 How did you get to the park?
2 Who did you go with?
3 What did you do there?
4 Which animals did you see?
5 Why did you go there?

a I went with my family.
b Because the park is lovely in the spring.
c Some deer and a fox.
d I went to a national park.
e We walked a lot and saw some animals.
f We went by car.

2 Order the questions.

you / Which / visit? / did / countries   *Which countries did you visit?*
1 go? / When / he / did
2 you / Did / see / on / the / TV? / weather
3 did / animals / the / disappear? / Why
4 people / Where / the / live? / did
5 TV / Did / like / they / programme? / the
6 How / we / did / long / stay?
7 yesterday? / eat / What / she / did /
8 good / everyone / Did / time? / a / have

3 Underline the wrong word in each line, then correct it.

Where did you <u>went</u> last night?   *go*
1 Did you have a pet when you were little? Yes, I had.
2 What did you had? A cat.
3 Why name did you give it? Snowy.
4 What had it look like? It was white.
5 Does it eat fish? Yes, it did. It liked fish a lot.
6 What did it sleep? On my bed.
7 Did it die of old age? Yes, it died.

Present continuous

4 Make full sentences using the present continuous.

I / read / book   *I'm reading a book.*
1 You / have / breakfast
2 They / visit / Jordan
3 She / take / photographs
4 We / buy / ticket
5 I / sit on / train
6 The train / leave / platform
7 She / talk / phone.
8 They / write / report

5 Complete the sentences with the best verb from the box and make it negative.

He *'s not watching* the football.

visit	feel	watch	stay	look	study	take	sit	wear

1 You _____ Russian.
2 We _____ the museum today.
3 She _____ a coat.
4 They _____ in a hotel.
5 I _____ cold.
6 He _____ on the bus.
7 We _____ a boat trip.
8 They _____ at the map.

6 Match a question to an answer.

Are you working at the weekend?
1 Are you learning English?
2 Is he visiting the palace?
3 Are they meeting in Brussels?
4 Are we paying for this trip?
5 Is she travelling by plane?
6 Is the train going to Moscow?

a No, he isn't.
b No, they aren't.
c Yes, we are.
d Yes, it is.
e No, I'm not.
f Yes, I am.
g No, she isn't.

Units 14 & 15

Describing nouns

- Both adjectives and nouns can describe nouns. They both go before the main noun: adjective / noun + main noun
  blue painting
  street art
- If there is both an adjective and a noun the adjective comes first:
  lovely chocolate cake

can

- We use **can** to talk about ability.
- Form the positive sentences with subject pronoun + **can** + verb:

Positive		
I	I **can**	
you	You **can**	
he/she/it	He/She/It **can**	speak French.
we	We **can**	play tennis.
you	You **can**	
they	They **can**	

- Form the negative with **not**:

Negative		
I	I **can't**	
you	You **can't**	
he/she/it	He/She/It **can't**	speak French
we	We **can't**	play tennis
you	You **can't**	
they	They **can't**	

- To make questions, put **can** first:
  They can speak French. *Can they speak French?*
- We usually use short answers:
  Yes, they can speak French. *Yes, they can.*

be going to (future)

- **be going to** is used for making predictions about the future.
- Form the positive with subject pronoun + **be** + **going to** + verb:

Positive			
I	I'm		
you	You're		
he/she/it	He's/She's/It's	**going to**	pass the exam.
we	We're		
you	You're		
they	They're		

- Form the negative with **not**:

Negative			
I	I'm not		
you	You're not		
he/she/it	He's/She's/It's not	**going to**	pass the exam.
we	We're not		
you	You're not		
they	They're not		

- To make questions, put the verb **be** first:
  You're going to be late. *Are you **going to** be late?*
- We usually use short answers:
  Yes, I'm going to be late. *Yes, I am.*

Units 14 & 15 Exercises

Describing nouns

1 Put the underlined words in the correct order (adjective + noun + main noun).

I don't like that street painting large. *I don't like that large street painting.*

1 He lives in a country small house.
2 She has a blue bike mountain.
3 That's a table big kitchen.
4 This is a station new bus.
5 What a match football boring.
6 She works at the local farm flower.

can

2 Write positive (+) or negative (-) sentences.

He / play the guitar. (-) *He can't play the guitar.*

1 We / swim (+)
2 She / ride a horse (-)
3 You / generate electricity with this gadget (+)
4 I / speak Arabic (-)
5 They / drive (-)
6 My computer / download music (+)

3 Complete the questions with the best verb from the box. Complete the short answers.

cook   paint   record   ~~speak~~   take   understand   use

you / Russian? ___*Can you speak Russian?*___   Yes, ___*I can*___

1 you / Italian food?
_____ Yes, _____
2 they / a computer?
_____ No, _____
3 your mp3 player / conversations?
_____ Yes, _____
4 your mobile phone / pictures?
_____ No, _____
5 he / science?
_____ No, _____
6 she / pictures?
_____ Yes, _____

be going to (future)

4 Change the sentences as shown.

He's going to get a new job. (+ ⟶ ?)
Is he going to get a new job?

1 It's going to be a nice day. (+ ⟶ -)
2 They aren't going to be happy. (- ⟶ +)
3 We're going to make a lot of money. (+ ⟶ -)
4 She's going to fail the exam. (+ ⟶ ?)
5 Are Liverpool going to win this year? (? ⟶ +)
6 She's going to marry Peter. (+ ⟶ ?)

5 Look at the table about the top 10 languages used on the internet. Match the beginnings and endings of the sentences.

In the future I think …

   there are going to be more Japanese sites
1 English language sites
2 Chinese sites
3 there are going to be more Portuguese sites
4 there aren't going to be
5 the top ten languages
6 there are going to be

a are always going to be second.
b any Swedish sites in the top ten.
c more and more people using the internet.
d are always going to be number one.
e than Spanish ones.
f than French or German ones.
g are always going to be about the same.

2009 (users in millions)		2008 (users in millions)	
English 478.4	German 64.5	English 430.8	Arabic 59.9
Chinese 383.6	Arabic 50.4	Chinese 276.2	Portuguese 58.2
Spanish 136.5	Russian 45.2	Spanish 124.7	Korean 34.8
Japanese 96	Korean 37.4	Japanese 94.0	Italian 34.7
French 79	Other languages 289.6	French 68.2	Other languages 220.9
Portuguese 73	Total million users: 1734	German 61.2	Total million users: 1463.6

Audioscript

Unit 1

Track 1.01
A: Hello. I'm Tom.
B: Hi. I'm Liz.
C: Hello. I'm Atul.
D: Hi. I'm Steve.
E: Hi. I'm Sasha.
F: Hello. I'm Pam.

Track 1.02
A: Hello. I'm Tom. I'm from London.
B: Hi. I'm Liz. I'm from Sydney.
C: Hello. I'm Atul. I'm from Mumbai.
D: Hi. I'm Steve. I'm from Cape Town.
E: Hi. I'm Sasha. I'm from New York.
F: Hello. I'm Pam. I'm from Toronto.

Track 1.04
A: Hi. I'm Lesley.
B: Lesley? Can you spell that?
A: L-E-S-L-E-Y
B: L-E-S-L-E-Y
A: That's right. I'm from Torquay.
B: Can you spell that?
A: T-O-R-Q-U-A-Y
B: T-O-R-Q-U-A-Y
A: That's right.
B: I'm Pedro.

Track 1.07
1 **A:** Name?
  B: Brown. B-R-O-W-N.
2 **A:** Name?
  B: Ball. B-A-L-L.
3 **A:** Can you spell that?
  B: C-L-A-R-K.
4 **A:** Can you spell your name?
  B: Barker. B-A-R-K-E-R.
5 **A:** Can you spell that, please?
  B: J-A-N-E-S. Janes.

Track 1.12
a one, two, three, five
b four, five, six, eight
c two, three, four, six
d six, seven, nine, ten
e nine, eight, seven, five
f five, three, two, one

Track 1.13
1 Manchester United 3, Liverpool 2
2 Yeah! Six! One, two, three, four, five, six!
3 **A:** Good morning.
  B: 2-1-3 please.
  A: 213. Here you are.
4 eight… three… four… one… nine… That's it … Oh no!
5 Four, five, two … six, nine, eight, eight.

Track 1.14
1 520751
2 C3 1XQ
3 L5R 3F6
4 GA 31302
5 115123

Unit 2

Track 1.20
1 **A:** Hello. I'm Lucian.
  B: Are you from France?
  A: No, I'm not. I'm English.
2 **A:** Hi. My name's Maria.
  B: Are you Italian?
  A: No, I'm not. I'm Spanish.
3 **A:** We're Olga and Tatiana.
  B: Are you German?
  A: No, we're not. We're Russian.

Track 1.21
1
A: Are you from Europe?
B: No, I'm not.
A: Are you married?
B: Yes, I am.
A: Are you a student?
B: No, I'm not.

Track 1.22
2
A: Are you from Europe?
B: Yes, I am.
A: Are you married?
B: Yes, I am.
A: Are you a student?
B: No, I'm not.

Track 1.23
3
A: Are you from Europe?
B: No, I'm not.
A: Are you married?
B: No, I'm not.
A: Are you a student?
B: Yes, I am.

Track 1.28
1 **A:** Bye
  B: Bye
  A: Oh…
  C: Come over here. What are these?
  A: Oh, they're my keys!
  C: OK.

Track 1.29
2 **A:** Passport! What's your name?
  B: Smith, Jean Smith.
  A: Where are you from?
  B: I'm Canadian. I'm from Vancouver.
  A: OK.
  B: Thank you.

Track 1.30
3 **A:** Is this your car?
  B: Er… Yes, it is.
  A: What's the number?
  B: Um… JGK 869D.
  A: Where are you from?
  B: I'm Polish. I'm from Warsaw.
  A: What's your address?
  B: The Royal Hotel.
  A: OK, thank you.
  B: Thank you!

Track 1.31
4 **A:** Open, please! Are these your bags?
  B: Yes, yes they are.
  A: Where are you from?
  B: We're French. We're from Lyon.
  A: What's that?
  B: It's our dog.
  A: OK, thank you.
  B: Thank you!

Track 1.34
eleven
twelve
thirteen
fourteen
fifteen
sixteen
seventeen
eighteen
nineteen
twenty

Track 1.35
1 **A:** What's your address?
  B: 18 Oxford Road.
  A: What's your postcode?
  B: L13 3PQ.

Track 1.36
2 **A:** What's your address?
  B: 20 King Street.
  A: What's your postcode?
  B: BS17 5TW.

Track 1.37
3 **A:** What's your address?
  B: 14b London Road.
  A: What's your postcode?
  B: M16 1A.

🎵 Track 1.38

4 **A:** What's your address?
  B: 15 Park Street.
  A: What's your postcode?
  B: NW11 4PT.

🎵 Track 1.40

1 My name is Pilar, I am from Spain. Uh, from Madrid.

🎵 Track 1.41

2 My name is Al-Mutasem Billa and my surname is Alam. I come from Saudi and I'm from a city, it's called Jeddah.

🎵 Track 1.42

3 So, my name is Marc, I come from France. More specifically, from a city called Lyon.

🎵 Track 1.43

4 My name's Dorothy Robertson. I'm from Alloa, Scotland.

🎵 Track 1.44

5 My name's Mireille Yanow. I'm from Diamond Bar, California, in the United States.

🎵 Track 1.47

Hi. My name's Tina. This is my English class. This is Gloria. She's from Argentina. The other students are from Spain. This is Pedro. He's from Granada. And Carmen and Luis are from Madrid. Our teacher's name is Max and he's from Manchester.

Unit 3

🎵 Track 1.51

1 Louise, Australia
  A: How many people are in your family?
  B: Four.

🎵 Track 1.52

2 Sulayman, Gambia
  A: Sulayman, how many people are in your family?
  B: In my family? Nine.

🎵 Track 1.53

3 Torsten, Germany
  A: Torsten – what about your family? Is it big?
  B: No, only two – me and my wife.

🎵 Track 1.54

4 Noriko, Japan
  A: How many people are in your family?
  B: Three.

🎵 Track 1.55

5 Hasna, Morocco
  A: So Hasna, how many people are in your family?
  B: Six. My mother and father, my sister and her husband. My niece – that's my sister's daughter, and me.

Unit 4

🎵 Track 1.64

1 My house number is 42.
2 I'm 27 years old.
3 There are 18 people in the class.
4 My grandmother is 64 years old.

🎵 Track 1.66

In this mall there are 6 floors for shopping and a big car park with 4 floors for cars. There are many interesting shops and there's a big supermarket. But it's not just for shopping; there are 48 restaurants and a cinema with 11 screens.

🎵 Track 1.69

1 **A:** How much is this?
  B: £24.
2 **A:** How much is the camera?
  B: $99.
3 **A:** Excuse me.
  B: Yes.
  A: How much is this pen?
  B: That's €1.30 please.
4 **A:** Hello.
  B: Hi.
  A: How much is this book, please?
  B: Let's see – er, £6.49.
  A: Thanks.

🎵 Track 1.76

1 How many restaurants are there in the picture?
2 Is there a hotel?
3 How many banks are there?
4 How much is the CD player?
5 How much is milk?
6 Is there a car park?
7 Is there a music shop?

Unit 5

🎵 Track 2.02

Jim
I work in a shop. It's a small shop. It's open every day. It's OK, but it's a bit boring.

🎵 Track 2.03

David
I work outdoors on a farm. It's a good job, but it's a difficult job too.

🎵 Track 2.04

Ingrid
I work for VSO, I'm a volunteer and I work in China. I'm a teacher. I work in a school. There are 12 teachers in the school. There isn't a lot of money but it's a very interesting job.

🎵 Track 2.05

Maria
I work in a restaurant. It's a cheap restaurant and it's very popular! There are a lot of people every day so it's very busy!

🎵 Track 2.06

Richard
I work for a big company in the centre of town. There are 150 people in the company. I work in an office. There are 19 people in the office with me. They're very friendly.

🎵 Track 2.07

Julie
I'm a volunteer for VSO. I work in a hospital. It's a good job, but it's very busy.

🎵 Track 2.08

swimming
running
table tennis
cricket
basketball
American football
football

🎵 Track 2.09

1 In most of South America, Africa and Europe, football is the national sport.
2 In India, Pakistan and Australia, cricket is the most popular sport.
3 In the United States the national sport is football – American football.
4 In China, table tennis is very popular.

🎵 Track 2.12

capoeira
ski-jumping
dancing
judo
motorbike racing

🎵 Track 2.13

1 Mireille, US
I love sports. Well, some sports I like. I like watching football and I like swimming.

🎵 Track 2.14

2 Christina, Germany
Yes, I do. My favourite sport is capoeira. It's a kind of Brazilian dance.

Audioscript

Track 2.15

3 Francesco, Italy
Well, I mean, yes, quite a bit. Not too much, but yes. I like motorbikes, so I like racing.

Track 2.16

4 Jolanta, Poland
Not football. I like ski-jumping the most.

Track 2.17

5 Eva, Switzerland
I do like sport, but not too much, not everything. I'm not a very sporty person in general. But what I do like doing is dancing.

Unit 6

Track 2.20

1 It's 6 o'clock. This is David Barnes with the news on Radio Cardiff.

Track 2.21

2 The train on Platform 4 is the 10.20 for London. 10.20 for London on Platform 4.

Track 2.22

3 At the third stroke it will be nine fifty-five precisely.

Track 2.23

4 A: Excuse me. What's the time?
B: Let's see – it's two thirty.
A: Sorry?
B: Two thirty.
A: OK. Thank you.

Track 2.25

I have a shower at 7.00 and then I have breakfast at about 7.30. I go to work at 8.15. I have lunch at 1.00. When I finish work I go to the gym – that's at about 6.15. After that I go home – at about 7.30. We have dinner at 8.00 and go to bed at 11.00.

Track 2.28

1 I phone my bank's call centre at night. I don't have time to phone in the day and at night it isn't so expensive.

Track 2.29

2 I like my job because it's just me and my car. And I like working nights. There's no traffic. My wife doesn't like it because I work all night and come home in the morning.

Track 2.30

3 I don't work normal hours, I work nights in a hospital. I like my job, but we don't have time to see other people. All my friends are nurses too!

Track 2.31

4 My supermarket doesn't close at night. 24-hour shopping? I think it's great. You don't spend hours in the shop. There's no one there – it's very quiet.

Unit 7

Track 2.41

A: What's the name of the site?
B: Great Smoky Mountains National Park.
A: Where is it?
B: It's in the south of the US – Tennessee and North Carolina.
A: How much is it?
B: Nothing! The park is free.
A: Wow, and when is it open?
B: It's open all day, every day.
A: What are the main attractions?
B: The park is great for walking. There are over 500 km of walks. The mountains are very popular and the fishing is good too!
A: When is a good time to visit?
B: Well, it's very busy in the summer. Spring and fall are good seasons to visit. And the trees are beautiful in the fall.
A: Great. Thanks!

Unit 8

Track 2.53

Katerina, Italy
I always, always every day have breakfast at 8 o'clock in the morning with my family, coffee is very important to wake us up and also some biscuits and some croissant with marmalade.

Track 2.54

Abdul, Saudi Arabia
I eat dinner sometimes, but the main meal for me is lunch which is rice with lamb or chicken.

Track 2.55

Ryusuke, Japan
I usually have er… dinner – for example I eat pasta and pizza and also Japanese traditional food such as sushi, Japanese omelettes and so on.

Track 2.56

Omar, Saudi Arabia
Usually I like to eat rice. We eat it for lunch time. It's so simple – rice and chicken, lamb and some vegetable with it.

Track 2.57

Francesco, Italy
Well, we're Italian so usually we eat pasta – that's the best thing we can find in Italy.

Unit 9

Track 2.61

Part 1
G'day! I live in Coober Pedy. This is a town in South Australia. It's in the desert and it's very hot in the summer! I live in an underground house. An underground house is great because it's never very hot or very cold. Come on in!

Track 2.62

Part 2
This is the kitchen. We have a fridge and a cooker of course. We eat in here so there's a table and chairs too. The living room is next to the kitchen, with a sofa, more chairs … There are lots of lamps because there are no windows.
And this is the bathroom. We have a shower but no bath. It's fun living in an underground house!

Track 2.63

And this is the bedroom. We have a bed of course, and a small table next to the bed. There aren't any windows but there's a lamp on the table. Oh and our cat is under the bed!

Unit 10

Track 2.70

Ancient Egypt was very important from 3150 to 35 BC. The ancient Egyptians were fantastic architects and there were many wonderful pyramids and temples.
Agriculture was very important and the typical food for normal Egyptians was bread and vegetables.
We have examples today of Egyptian writing and numbers. There were symbols for numbers one and ten, but no symbols for numbers two to nine.
Animals were very important to Egyptian families and many families had a pet. Cats were very popular.

Track 2.71

A: So Jackie, you were in Cairo last month. What was that like?
B: Fantastic, Mike! Here, have a look at my photos.
A: OK, oh so was this your hotel?
B: Yes, it was. It was the first modern hotel in Cairo. It was great! The hotel was next to the Egyptian museum, the one with King Tutankhamen inside. That was wonderful!
A: Was the food good?
B: Yes it was. It was delicious. This was my first meal in Cairo. There was rice, meat, vegetables and bread in lots of different bowls.

A: Wow, the Pyramids!

B: Yes, they were fantastic, of course. Look at me on the horse! It was very old and slow! There weren't any other tourists because I was there very early in the morning – and it was cold! It wasn't hot in January in the morning! OK, so this was Ali, my guide.

A: Ali, right. So, were the people nice?

B: Well, Ali was very nice – all the Egyptians were very friendly.

A: Cairo's a very big city. Was the traffic bad?

B: Oh yes, that was terrible. There were so many cars, and buses and taxis. The taxis were awful – they weren't expensive but they were very hot and very slow. It was really noisy too. But at night the river Nile was really beautiful.

A: So, a good trip?

B: Oh yes!

🔊 Track 2.75

Part 1: Remember Unit 10
1 What was the religion of the Khmer?
2 What was the typical food for the Khmer?
3 How many days were in the Mayan month?
4 What was the important food for the Mayans?
5 What film was made in Tikal?

Part 2: Odd one out
1 wonderful, fantastic, awful, delicious
2 fridge, cooker, table, shower
3 terrible, friendly, noisy, awful
4 Monday, Friday, weekend, Thursday
5 rent, was, go, see

Part 3: Where was ...
1 Where was Jackie in January?
2 Where was the film *Tomb Raider* made?
3 Where was Merv's underground house?
4 Where was Stanley Park?

Unit 11

🔊 Track 3.08

A: Is Christmas Day on the 24th of December?

B: No, it isn't. It's on the 25th of December.

🔊 Track 3.09

A: In China New Year's Day is in January or February.

B: Oh really? For me it's always the 1st of January.

🔊 Track 3.10

A: Is Valentine's Day in March?

B: No, it's in February. It's on the 14th of February.

🔊 Track 3.11

A: Australia Day? When's that?

B: It's on the 26th of January.

🔊 Track 3.12

A: I think Europe Day is on the 8th of May.

B: No, it isn't. It's on the 9th of May.

🔊 Track 3.15

Bea, England
A memorable year is 1998 because I went travelling round the world.

🔊 Track 3.16

Pilar, Spain
My important year is this year because I am living in London and I think that is very difficult for me because I am from Spain and the weather and the food is very different.

🔊 Track 3.17

Carmen, Spain
I think probably the most important year of my life was er... 2001 because it was the year before I started the university and it was a very hard year for me.

🔊 Track 3.18

Mireille, US
I think probably 2002 because that's the year I moved to the United Kingdom.

🔊 Track 3.19

Maria, Spain
I think a memorable year would be 2007 and that's because my son was born and so, life is very different now ... since then.

Unit 12

🔊 Track 3.22

A: Which country did it come from?

B: It came from Australia.

A: How big was it?

B: Well, it was very small. It was 3cm long.

A: Where did it live?

B: It lived in the mountains, next to small rivers.

A: Right, and what did it eat?

B: It ate insects.

A: How did it live?

B: The frog was very busy in the day. It looked for food and went into the water a lot. It also sat in the sun. At night it went under rocks to sleep.

A: So why did it disappear?

B: Well, we don't know. Some people think there was a problem with the frog's habitat.

A: And when did it disappear?

B: There were a lot of frogs in the early 1970s but it disappeared in 1979.

🔊 Track 3.23

A: When I was little our family had a donkey.

B: Did it have a name?

A: Yes, it was Ronaldo.

B: What did it eat?

A: It ate carrots and grass.

B: Where did it live?

A: It lived in the garden.

B: Did you like it?

A: Yes, I did.

🔊 Track 3.26

A: Did you see that TV series about that man ... oh what's his name ... Bruce Parry?

B: Bruce Parry? Who's he?

A: He's a TV presenter. He made this incredible series called *Tribe*.

B: What did he do?

A: He lived with tribes ...

B: Tribes? Where? Where did he go?

A: He went to lots of different countries – Malaysia, Brazil, Russia, Tanzania ...

B: Are there tribes in all those places?

A: Yeah, it was fascinating.

B: Who did he go with?

A: Obviously he went with a TV production team.

B: Yeah OK. Where did he stay?

A: This is the interesting thing. He stayed with a family in the tribe.

B: All the time?

A: Yes, day and night – and he did everything they did.

B: Wow. How long did he stay? Two or three days?

A: No he stayed for a month.

B: A month? Wow. What food did he eat?

A: That was incredible. He had exactly the same food as the tribe – you saw him eat lots of strange food – insects, rats ...

B: Rats? That's horrible. But did he like it, did he have a good time?

A: I think so – the people were really friendly to him, but I think it was also quite difficult for him. Life in the tribe was quite hard.

B: It sounds really interesting ...

Audioscript

Unit 13

Track 3.33

If you want to go from London St Pancras to Paris, the Eurostar takes just 135 minutes. And if Brussels is your destination, then you can be there in 113 minutes. The train has a top speed of 300km per hour. The total number of passengers is 766 with 206 in first class and 560 in standard class. But what about tickets and prices? If you want to travel first class, your ticket will cost £260 but if that's too expensive you can buy a standard ticket for just £39.

Track 3.34

A: How was the meeting, Anne?
B: Fine, John, it went very well.
A: So, where are you now?
B: I'm at the train station and I'm just checking the timetable. I think the train leaves at 16.30 … Let me see, yes it does. OK, I'm at the ticket office now, speak later!

Track 3.35

B: Hi John, I have the ticket.
A: No problems, then?
B: No, none at all. I'm on the platform just waiting for the train now.
A: What time does the train arrive in Brussels?
B: About 7.30 this evening. John – the train's arriving now …

Track 3.36

B: Hi John. I'm just arriving in Belgium.
A: How's the Eurostar?
B: Great – the seats are very comfortable! I'm glad I took the train.
A: I hope you aren't working now.
B: Oh no, I'm reading a book.
A: OK, call me tonight from the hotel …

Track 3.37

A: Mr Peeters? Hello, this is Anne, Anne Ross.
B: Good evening Anne. Welcome to Brussels!
A: Thank you, but I have a problem. I understand that someone from the office is meeting me at the station.
B: Yes, that's right.
A: Well, I'm waiting but there's no-one here.
B: Don't worry, I'm coming to meet you now.
A: Great, I'm waiting next to platform 6. See you soon.

Track 3.41

A: Hello. Is this the tour bus?
B: Yes, this is the Moscow City Bus Tour.
A: OK, great, one adult please.
B: That's 800 roubles please …
Good morning Ladies and Gentlemen and welcome to Moscow City Bus Tours. My name's Katya and I'm your guide this morning. This morning we're visiting the most important sights in Moscow including the Bolshoi Theatre and Red Square, so have your cameras ready! Please ask me …
OK Ladies and Kentlemen. The building you're looking at is the Tretyakov Gallery, one of the most important art galleries in Moscow. If you only visit one museum in Moscow, visit this gallery …
A: Oh hi love … I'm fine. I'm seeing the city on one of those, er tourist buses … Cold? No, it's not cold. I'm not wearing my coat anyway … How about you? What are you doing? … Yeah? Oh, OK, I have to go – we're arriving at the Kremlin palace. OK, see you later, bye.

Unit 14

Track 3.49

A: I really like this painting.
B: Me too.
A: I like it because there's a lot of yellow in it.
B: Really? My favourite colour is blue.
A: The painting is of a street, er … in France.
B: Yes, I think so.
A: There's a café and there are some chairs and tables in the street. There are some people in the café. It's in the evening.
B: Really? I don't agree – I think it's at night.

Track 3.52

The One Laptop Per Child organisation started in 2005. It helps children in developing countries. It gives the children special computers to help their education. Children in several countries, including Peru, Uruguay, Cambodia, Ethiopia and Afghanistan are using the special XO computers.
The XO computer has a special design. It can operate with only 2 watts of electricity and you can read the screen in the sun. It only costs about $180.
The children can read, write and play games. They can also connect to the internet. The computer has a camera and microphone so the children can take photos and have a video conference. Are there any problems? Well, the computers are slow to start and you can't use CDs or DVDs. But the main problem is politics; some governments don't want to spend money on the project and some computer companies aren't happy about the cheap price of the XO computer.

Track 3.56

Nicole, Switzerland
So my favourite gadget is the mobile phone.

Track 3.57

Dorothy, Scotland
My favourite gadget is a food processor because I enjoy cooking.

Track 3.58

Abdul, Saudi Arabia
My favourite is my mobile phone.

Track 3.59

Marc, France
One of my favourite gadgets, erm … my watch would be a gadget and it's my favourite one because it's useful to have a watch with you.

Track 3.60

Nicole, Switzerland
I can listen to music with my mobile phone and I can also take pictures when I have forgotten my camera.

Track 3.61

Dorothy, Scotland
I only have a very old mobile phone. I can make telephone calls and I can send text messages.

Track 3.62

Abdul, Saudi Arabia
I can send email and take photos.

Track 3.63

Marc, France
So what can I do with my mobile phone? Well, basically to contact other people. That's what I do with my mobile phone.

Unit 15

Track 3.66

1   A half plus a quarter is three-quarters.
2   Fifty percent of ninety is forty-five.
3   Eighty-four is double forty-two.
4   Forty-seven is half of ninety-four.

Track 3.67

A: Gemma, you come from Jersey which is a small island. I know it's near France – do people speak both English and French?
B: No, English is the main language, everyone speaks English. However,

there are groups of Portuguese, Polish, French and Kenyans who speak their native languages.

A: Right.

B: There is another language called Jèrriais. It's a local language that people spoke in the past.

A: So do many people speak that today?

B: No, not really. There are about 90,000 people in Jersey and less than 4% speak Jèrriais – and it's mainly older people. Perhaps about 15% can understand some of it.

A: Now I know many people are learning Jèrriais. Why is that?

B: Well, for two reasons. The first is to keep the language and the culture of Jersey, and the second is for fun.

A: What about the young people – are they interested?

B: A little, there are classes at some schools now. The government is trying to make more young people learn it.

A: A language disappears every two weeks – is Jèrriais going to disappear?

B: I hope not. No, I think it's going to be here for some time.

A: And what about you – do you speak Jèrriais?

B: No, I don't. But I'm going to start classes next year.

Track 3.68

1   They didn't do their homework. The teacher's going to be angry.

2   Arabic is a difficult language. I'm going to have problems learning it.

3   Jane and Tom are moving to Tokyo. They're going to learn Japanese.

4   You didn't work very hard. You're going to fail the exam.

Track 3.69

There are about 7000 languages in the world and the language with the most native speakers is Chinese. Mandarin Chinese is also becoming a very popular foreign language with about 30 million students round the world.

For many parents, English is a very important language and some children start learning it very young. In Japan, about 21% of five-year-olds are already going to English conversation classes and 90% of European schoolchildren study English.

English is very important in other countries but what about British people? Are they good language learners? No, they're not. Only 5% of British adults can count to 20 in another language.

Irregular verbs

Infinitive	Past simple	Past participle
be	was/were	been
beat	beat	beaten
become	became	become
begin	began	begun
bend	bent	bent
bet	bet	bet
bite	bit	bitten
blow	blew	blown
break	broke	broken
bring	brought /brɔːt/	brought /brɔːt/
build /bɪld/	built /bɪlt/	built /bɪlt/
burn	burnt/burned	burnt/burned
burst	burst	burst
buy /baɪ/	bought /bɔːt/	bought /bɔːt/
can	could /kʊd/	(been able)
catch	caught /kɔːt/	caught /kɔːt/
choose	chose	chosen
come	came	come
cost	cost	cost
cut	cut	cut
deal /diːl/	dealt /delt/	dealt /delt/
dig	dug	dug
do	did	done
draw	drew	drawn
dream	dreamt/dreamed	dreamt/dreamed
drink	drank	drunk
drive	drove	driven
eat	ate	eaten
fall	fell	fallen
feed	fed	fed
feel	felt	felt
fight	fought /fɔːt/	fought /fɔːt/
find	found	found
fly	flew	flown
forget	forgot	forgotten
forgive	forgave	forgiven
freeze	froze	frozen
get	got	got
give	gave	given
go	went	gone/been
grow	grew	grown
hang	hung/hanged	hung/hanged
have	had	had
hear	heard /hɜːd/	heard /hɜːd/
hide	hid	hidden
hit	hit	hit
hold	held	held
hurt /hɜːt/	hurt /hɜːt/	hurt /hɜːt/
keep	kept	kept
kneel	knelt/kneeled	knelt/kneeled
know	knew /njuː/	known
lay	laid	laid
lead	led	led
learn /lɜːn/	learnt/learned	learnt/learned
leave	left	left
lend	lent	lent
let	let	let

Infinitive	Past simple	Past participle
lie	lay	lain
light	lit	lit
lose	lost	lost
make	made	made
mean	meant /ment/	meant /ment/
meet	met	met
must	had to	(had to)
pay	paid	paid
put	put	put
read	read /red/	read /red/
ride	rode	ridden
ring	rang	rung
rise	rose	risen
run	ran	run
say	said /sed/	said /sed/
see	saw /sɔː/	seen
sell	sold	sold
send	sent	sent
set	set	set
shake	shook	shaken
shine	shone	shone
shoot	shot	shot
show	showed	shown
shrink	shrank	shrunk
shut	shut	shut
sing	sang	sung
sink	sank	sunk
sit	sat	sat
sleep	slept	slept
slide	slid	slid
smell	smelt/smelled	smelt/smelled
speak	spoke	spoken
spell	spelt/spelled	spelt/spelled
spend	spent	spent
spill	spilt/spilled	spilt/spilled
split	split	split
spoil	spoilt/spoiled	spoilt/spoiled
spread	spread	spread
stand	stood	stood
steal	stole	stolen
stick	stuck	stuck
swear	swore	sworn
swell	swelled	swollen/swelled
swim	swam	swum
take	took /tʊk/	taken
teach	taught /tɔːt/	taught /tɔːt/
tear	tore	torn
tell	told	told
think	thought /θɔːt/	thought /θɔːt/
throw	threw	thrown
understand	understood	understood
wake	woke	woken
wear	wore /wɔː/	worn
win	won /wʌn/	won /wʌn/
write	wrote	written

Macmillan Education
Between Towns Road, Oxford OX4 3PP
A division of Macmillan Publishers Limited
Companies and representatives throughout the world

ISBN 978-0-230-03282-8

Original design by Barbara Mercer and Katie Stephens
Page make-up by eMC Design Limited
Illustrated by Jonathan Burton, Mathew Hams, Piers Sandford, Peter Cornwell, eMC Design and Barbara Mercer
Picture research by Sally Cole, Perseverance Works Limited
Cover design by Barbara Mercer
Cover credit: Cover photos (front, spine, back): By permission of the Museum of the History of Science, University of Oxford/Keiko Ikeuchi.

Authors' acknowledgements
First and foremost we would like to thank Rafael Alarcón-Gaeta and the editorial and design teams at Macmillan: Nick Sheard, Stephanie Parker, Barbara Mercer, Stig Vatland, Sarah O'Driscoll, Claire Sparkes and Carole Hughes.We would also like to thank Jo Greig, Matt Kay and the rest of the marketing team. There are of course many other people whose efforts have helped make a book we are really proud of, in particular Robert Campbell and Matt Beesley for their work on the eWorkbook and Fran Watkins and Rob Metcalf for their contribution to the Teacher's Book.

Kate would like to dedicate this book to her mother Hazel for all her love and encouragement over the years.

Jackie would like to dedicate this book to her parents, Pam and Robert, with love and thanks.

The authors and publishers would like to thank all the teachers and consultants who have piloted and reviewed the material. Particular thanks go to the following people: Andrea Córdova, Susana Flores (Anglo Multimedia School of English, Haedo, Buenos Aires, Argentina); Ma. Cristina Maggi, Ma. Cristina Buero de Chinton (Friends' School of English, Adrogué, Buenos Aires, Argentina); Mirta Zampini, Aldana Anchorena, Elizabeth Rainieri, Ma. Soledad D. Mangiarotti, Pamela Sabrina Pecorelli (IECI, Haedo, Buenos Aires, Argentina); Alejandro Jorge Listrani (Cultural Inglesa de Palermo, Ciudad Autónoma de Buenos Aires, Argentina); Lilian Itzicovitch Leventhal (Potential/Colegio I.L.Peretz, São Paulo, Brazil); Ana Maria Miranda (Cultura Inglesa Ribeirão Preto, Ribeirão Preto, Brazil); Magali de Moraes Menti (FACCAT - Escola Municipal Lauro Rodrigues, Porto Alegre, Brazil); Simone Sarmento (PUCRS, Porto Alegre, Brazil); Laura Lee Lehto (Cultura Inglesa, Fortaleza, Brazil); Viviane Cristine Silva Grossklauss, Analice Sandovetti (Cultura Inglesa Jundiaí, Jundiaí, Brazil); Celia Aguiar de Almeida Costa (Cultura Inglesa de Juiz de Fora, Brazil); Corina Celia Machado Correa (Associação Alumni - São Paulo, Brazil); Jane Godwin, (The Four, São Carlos, Brazil); Caroline Toubia (The Holy Family School, Jesuite, Egypt); Amany Shawkey, Heidi Omara (Macmillan Publishers Ltd, Egypt) Caroline Franz , Dana Jelinkova (MVHS Muenchner Volkshochschule, Munich, Germany); Irene Rodriguez, Haydee Gutierrez Palafox, Antonio Morales de la Barrera, Javier Ramos de Hoyos (The Anglo Mexican Foundation, Mexico City, Mexico); Viviana Caruso de Curtius (freelance author and consultant, Mexico City, Mexico); Emma Dominguez (Academic Studies Manager, The Anglo Mexican Foundation, Mexico City, Mexico); Katarzyna Rogalińska-Gajewska (Archibald, Warsaw, Poland); Małgorzata Woźniak, Dorota Pachwicewicz, Agnieszka Kilanowska (Centrum Językowe 'Euroclub', Gdańsk, Poland); Fabiola Georgiana Hosu (Little London School and Nursery School, Dimitrie Cantemir University, Bucharest, Romania); Lydia B. Korzheva (Diplomatic Academy, Moscow, Russia); Ludmila A. Pokrovskaya (Russian Academy of Foreign Trade, Moscow, Russia); Olga S. Petrischeva (Moscow State University of International Relations, Moscow, Russia); Albina Valieva (The international Language School 'Denis School', Moscow, Russia); Karen Dyer, Cathy Harris, Frank Hodgkins (International House, Madrid, Spain); Carlos Trueba (E.O.I. Villaverde, Madrid, Spain); Patricia Plaza Arregui, (E.O.I. Malaga, Spain); Maria Esther Álvarez Rico (E.O.I. Sagunto, Valencia, Spain); Burcu Tezcan Ünal (Bilgi University, Istanbul, Turkey); Dr. F. Ilke Buyukduman (Ozyegin University, Istanbul, Turkey); Sarah Shaw (The British Council, Chiang Mai, Thailand); Aomboon Burutphakdee (Payap University, Chiang Mai, Thailand); Claudia Edwards (London School of English, London, UK); Sally Jones (Regent Oxford, Oxford, UK); Katherine Griggs (Community English School Oxfordshire Adult Learning, Oxford, UK).

A special thank you to Jackie Halsall, Sarah Paterson and all the staff and students at Eckersley, Oxford and Regent, Oxford for all their help with Global voices.

Kate would like to thank her 2007-2008 AO Senior students at International House Madrid.

Jackie would like to give special thanks to Richard Cain, Lina Marji and all the teachers at the British Council Amman.

The authors and publishers would like to thank the following for providing information to be included in the book: Merv Richards; Salim and Cathy at Wild Things Safaris; Jemma Jelley; the staff at VSO.

The authors and publishers would like to thank the following for permission to reproduce their photographs:

Alamy Images/Ace Stock Ltd p78(br), Alamy/J.Arnold Photography p73(l), Alamy/Blitzjp p39(tr), Alamy/M.Booth p38(ml), Alamy/J.Bower p8(l), Alamy/J.Butler p80(ml), Alamy/R.Cousins p63(b), Alamy/R. Cracknell 01/classic p62(bml), Alamy/dbimages p84(tr), Alamy/S. Denson p26(ml), Alamy/F.Fossez p84(mr), Alamy/T.Gartside p38(mr), Alamy/Ilian Studio pp54(br), 54(ml), Alamy/P.Jordan p93(tl), Alamy/P. Kingsley p55(bl), Alamy/R.Levine p26(mb), Alamy/E.Linssen p27(br), Alamy/I.Nolan pp54(mbr), 55(ml), Alamy/S.Rawles p35(tr), Alamy/H. Rogers pp27(t), 29, 58, Alamy/F.Wood p85(l), Alamy/J.Woodhouse p8(r), Alamy/World Pictures p79(t), Alamy/A.Van Zandbergen p84(ml); **Press Association**/AP/N.H.Guan p97(l), Press Association/AP/N.Carson p101(l); Aurora p56(tr); **Bananastock** p104(ml), 104(mr); **BBC**/Blast Films/J.Clay p7(b); **BrandX** pp 25, 35(tl), 72(tr), 104(bml); **Comstock Images** pp48(water), 104(btl); **Corbis**/R.Benali p32(bl), Corbis/H.Benser p78(t), Corbis/A.F.Bradley p76(b), Corbis/J.Finley p69(bl), Corbis/The Gallery Collection p51(b), Corbis/S.Crasto p39(br), Corbis/M.K.Daly p32(br), Corbis/M.Everton p32(tr), Corbis/O.Franken p78(ml), Corbis/C. Garratt p78(mr), Corbis/P.Ginter pp9(tl), 41, Corbis/J.Gollings p24(bl), Corbis/B.Harrington 111 p61, Corbis/R.Heffernan p32(tm), Corbis/A. Hofford p102(br), Corbis/J.Horner p69(tl), Corbis/A.Jones p63(t), Corbis/W.Kaehler p80(mr), Corbis/E.Kreutz p33(t), Corbis/J.Bower/ Loop Images p60(l), Corbis/S.Lupton p26(mr), Corbis/D.Mason p14(mr), Corbis/1888 The Starry Night by Vincent van Gogh Image by © The Gallery Collection p85(r), Corbis/1888 Cafe Terrace at Night by Vincent van Gogh Image by © Francis G. Mayer p85(m), Corbis/J.Mitchell p84(tl), Corbis/B.Radford p8(bml), Corbis/L.Quail p93(r), Corbis/ J.F.Raga p43(t), Corbis/P.Santos p74(l), Corbis/P.Souders pp72(tm), 77(tmr), Corbis/P.Turnley p68, Corbis/J.Vizcaino p56(tm); **Corbis** RF pp32(bmr), 35(tm), 35(bl), 48(cheese), 104(br), 104(m); **Foodpix** p62(bmr); **Fotolibra**/ S.Bernard p8(bm), Fotolibra/J.Egglestone 51(t), Fotolibra/J. Fowler p8(bmr), Fotolibra/M.Galan p39(bl); **Gallo Images** pp57, 87(bl); **Getty Images** p33(b), Getty/K.Basayev p91(b), Getty/Business Wire p86(tl), Getty/K.Desouki p62(tm), Getty/J.Fitzjones p54(tr), Getty/P. Hauser p6(r), Getty/G.Lawrence p80(t), Getty/National Geographic p62(bl), Getty/H.Neleman p96(r), Getty/O.Nikishin p80(bm), Getty/I. Pitalev p81, Getty/A.Smith/Workbook Stock p13(tr), Getty/Universal Images Group p92, Getty/C.Walsh p86(m); **Getty RF** pp22(l), 22(tr), 32(tl), 48(meat), 48(fish), 48(vegetables), 48(juice), 48(fruit), 48(icecream), 77(tl), 77(tml); **Goodshoot** pp62(br), 65; **Hulton Archive** pp24(l), 76(ml), 76(ml), 79(mr); **Iconica** p8(bl); **Image Bank** pp14(tr), 14(l), 19(b), 36(tr), 42(mr), 47(5), 78(bl), 83, 91(t); **Image Source** pp22(m), 22(bm), 37(m), p48(coffee), 104(bml), 104(tml), 104(btmr) 104(bmr); **John Foxx Images**

The author and publishers are grateful for permission to reprint the following copyright material:

The authors and publishers would like to thank the following for permission to reproduce the following copyright material:

VSO, *Voluntary Service Overseas* for details about volunteers, copyright © 2009 VSO;

Wild Things TZ Ltd for details about safaris, copyright © *Wild Things TZ Ltd*;

Merv Richards for details and quotations, reproduced with permission;

Euromonitor International for statistics from 'Top 150 City Destinations: London Leads the Way' by Caroline Bremner, 11 October 2007, http://www.euromonitor.com/Top_150_City_Destinations_London_Leads_the_Way copyright © Euromonitor International 2009;

One Laptop per Child for their logo, company and mission details, adapted from http://laptop.org/en/children/countries/index.shtml and http://wiki.laptop.org/go/Official_OLPC_FAQ;

Material about *Tata Nano car*, reproduced with permission of Tata Motors.

Map page 12 courtesy of www.theodora.com/maps <file://www.theodora.com/maps> , used with permission.

These materials may contain links for third party websites. We have no control over, and are not responsible for, the contents of such third party websites. Please use care when accessing them.

Every effort has been made to trace the copyright holders, but if any have been inadvertently overlooked, the publishers will be pleased to make the necessary arrangements at the first opportunity.

Printed in Thailand

2014 2013 2012 2011 2010
10 9 8 7 6 5 4 3 2